P9-DJL-191

Swim!

Walter Bond

Swim!

HOW A SHARK,
A SUCKERFISH,
AND A PARASITE
TEACH YOU LEADERSHIP,
MENTORING, AND NEXT-LEVEL SUCCESS

A BUSINESS FABLE

WILEY

Published by John Wiley & Sons, Inc., Hoboken, New Jersey.
Published simultaneously in Canada.

For general information on our other products and services or for technical support, please contact our Customer Care Department within the United States at (800) 762-2974, outside the United States at (317) 572-3993 or fax (317) 572-4002.

Wiley publishes in a variety of print and electronic formats and by print-on-demand. Some material included with standard print versions of this book may not be included in e-books or in print-on-demand. If this book refers to media such as a CD or DVD that is not included in the version you purchased, you may download this material at http://booksupport.wiley.com. For more information about Wiley products, visit www.wiley.com.

ISBN 9781119573562 (Hardcover)
ISBN 9781119573630 (ePDF)
ISBN 9781119573555 (ePub)

Cover design & Illustration: Paul McCarthy

Printed in the United States of America

V10010885_060619

I want to dedicate this book to the shark I am married to, Antoinette Mayo Bond. You have been with me and have stood by my side from day one in this business. The journey has had its ups and downs, but you have always been my shark and I love being your suckerfish. Thanks for believing in me and knowing which of my ideas are good and which of them suck. This book somehow squeezed past you, so either you weren't looking or it's going to be a bestseller. LOL!

Wesley Bond, thank you, son, for your frank feedback and getting into the book in the first place. Your feedback made us go back to the drawing board on a lot. This book is a part of you, too.

Kendall and Cori Bond, thanks for letting your dad share his ideas and thanks for being excited about every one of them. It must take real true love to sit through all my ramblings. I believe we did it this time.

Contents

1

The Reunion

Scotty was elbow-deep in a frozen air conditioner when his phone began to vibrate. He wiped his hands on his jeans and dug into his pocket for his phone. He didn't recognize the number, so he shoved the phone into his back pocket and leaned back into the icy air conditioner. A short, loud beep indicated he had a voicemail. Perplexed, Scotty lifted the phone to his ear to listen to the message.

"Scotty! Scotty, my man—hey, listen, this is Paul Gray! I'm here for the long weekend with my son, Zach. We came to pick up a little present I bought for myself at the marina near you and wanted to see if you'd like to head out for a little test drive on the water? Maybe do some fishing? Let me know, would love to catch up with ya!"

Paul's tone was the same as it had always been: upbeat, high-energy, confident. Scotty was a little confused as to why Paul Gray would be calling him to hang out. They hadn't spoken since high school more than 25 years ago, and even back then they weren't the best of friends, like they had been in middle school. A little present I bought for myself? Scotty replayed the message in his mind. Down at the marina? It was all a bit weird and very out of the blue, but Scotty was intrigued. He remembered seeing something online about Paul having a son right around the time Scotty and his high-school-sweetheart-turned-wife, CiCi, found out they were pregnant with Brittany, but that was almost 20 years ago.

Scotty was busy, so he tried to dismiss the idea and get back to work, but he was distracted by the phone call. What was good ol' Paul up to, and had he changed at all since high school? *If we did go out,* Scotty thought, *would we have anything in common? What would we talk about?* He worked and fumbled inside the frozen AC until it was up and running, and went to tell the kind old woman that he was done.

"Thank you, Scotty!" the old lady exclaimed as he explained that the AC was fixed and her house would be cooling off shortly.

"My pleasure. Call me if you need anything else!" Scotty said with a smile. As he walked out of the front door, he pulled her overflowing trashcans to the curb to be picked up by the garbage truck later that day. She was a widow, and he loved doing little household things for her that she couldn't do on her own. He started his truck and headed home for the day, Paul's message still replaying in his mind.

When he got home with a bag of CiCi's favorite takeout food, CiCi met him at the door with a big smile, just as she always had. He dropped the bag and wrapped her in a big bear hug, still in love with the way her hair smelled when she got out of the shower.

"Eat by the pool?" she asked, taking the bag and heading through the front entranceway of the home.

"Sounds good! I'll get the wineglasses and meet you out there," Scotty replied.

They sipped wine and ate orange chicken with chopsticks and looked out at the pool. The waterfall feature was his favorite, as it added a calming vibe to the entire outdoor area and was the perfect respite from the world. They chatted about their days, CiCi sharing stories about her "little rhinos," her affectionate name for the wild kindergarteners she was responsible for shaping and molding each day. As he tried not to bore her with tedious details about cooling coils and compressors, he remembered the phone call.

"Oh! I almost forgot!" he said as he put his wineglass down. "Guess who called me today?" he asked with a mouth full of lo mein.

CiCi shrugged.

"Paul Gray!"

"Paul? Why?" she asked, her eyebrows raised.

Scotty laughed. "Beats me. Said he was in town buying something down at the marina, wants to go fishing." Scotty analyzed CiCi's face for a reaction.

"That's random. When's the last time you guys talked?"

"Years. I may have sent him a congratulations note when his kid was born. Same age as Brittany."

"Wow. Are you gonna go?" she asked.

"I don't know. I wasn't, and then I thought about it and . . . I don't know."

"Think about it. Brittany will be here this weekend, she may be interested in going out on the boat—I mean, if he's bringing his kid . . ." CiCi suggested.

"I'll call him tomorrow about it. We'll see. More wine?" he asked, pouring the vintage cabernet into their glasses.

The next day was a busy one for Scotty. He decided that if he didn't call Paul as he drove into work, the day would get too busy and he would forget, so he commanded the Bluetooth in his car to call Paul. The phone rang twice.

"Scotty boy!" Paul's big, hefty voice said as he picked up the phone. "How are you, man?" Paul's smile was contagious, even over the phone.

"I'm good! How are you? Was happy to get your message yesterday. What's going on?" Scotty asked.

"Me and my boy, Zach, are in town in Fort Lauderdale picking up a little toy I bought for myself. Got a forty-two footer, center cabin, a real beauty. You free this weekend to take her out? I got enough gear. You got a kid, right? Bring him, too!"

"Wow, forty-two footer. That's not a little toy," Scotty said, and immediately regretted it. If this Paul was anything like high school Paul, that little comment just inflated his ego even more. "I have a daughter actually, she'll be in town this weekend and—"

"Bring her, too!" Paul interrupted. "We got plenty of lines, plenty of room. I went out a few months ago and saw a great white out there, man! What a sight. What do you say?" Paul asked, a little louder and more energetic than necessary. Scotty hesitated, but knew that if this Paul was anything like high school Paul, he wasn't going to take no for an answer.

"Yeah, that sounds great. Let's do it. I'm pulling into work now. Can you shoot me an email with the details tonight?" Scotty asked, putting the car in park.

"Yeah, yeah, yeah! I'll do that. Okay, cool. Looking forward to it, buddy!"

"Me too. Should be fun! I'll talk to you la—"

"Yep, talk to you soon. Bye bye!" and with that, it was silent.

Scotty smiled and shook his head. Seemed like Paul hadn't changed much since high school, and now Scotty was wondering what he was getting himself into.

Scotty pulled into the office building and jiggled the key in the front door. He switched on the lights and headed to his office. He sat down and flipped through his planner to today's date. First up: the 8 a.m. tech meeting. He loved these meetings, as they were sometimes the only part of the day where he could really connect with all the guys (and Tracey, their only female AC tech), and listen to their questions or concerns.

Tech meetings always made Scotty think about his very first 8 a.m. tech meeting with Drew, the founder of Shark's AC Repair Service, at the local Boys and Girls Club. Scotty's dad was a drinker before his mom died, and her death just sent him spiraling out of control. Scotty dreaded going home from school each day, on edge about whether it would be him or the living room wall that got the brunt of his father's grief-induced rage.

He loved these meetings, as they were sometimes the only part of the day where he could really connect with all the guys.

Not wanting to go home as a kid is how Scotty ended up in the backseat of the Jamesons' car, which is how he wound up in the back of a police car for the first time a few hours later. But that time would not be his last. Finally, a compassionate judge ruled that his poor choices were a result of his unstable home life, truancy, and his "extended periods of unsupervised time" and mandated that Scotty go straight to the Boys and Girls Club every day after school as alternative to juvenile detention. Scotty had been annoyed but thought anything was better than going home to his dad or juvie.

Scotty looked at the keepsakes on his desk. Front and center was a plaque Brittany had made for him for Father's Day with the Sacred Six engraved in silver. There was one photo of Brittany on her third birthday and one of CiCi in the passenger seat of his first car, one of CiCi and Scotty kissing on their wedding day, and one of Drew standing in front of a Shark's AC Repair Service truck surrounded by all of the techs. Someone must have said something funny because everyone was laughing. The picture was faded, but you could see the sparkle in Drew's eyes. Every time Scotty looked at this picture of Drew, he remembered with fondness the day he met him.

The evening bus had dropped Scotty off in front of the newly renovated Boys and Girls Club. He saw a few people he recognized from school walk in and saw that everyone was sitting down and eating dinner. His stomach rumbled, reminding him that he hadn't eaten in a while. *I'll just eat and then I'll go,* he thought to himself. Scotty seemed to be a pro at formulating an escape plan, always looking for a way to get out, escape, avoid. He was weighing his options as he stood on the sidewalk. He was about to turn around and leave, and then he saw CiCi, a beautiful senior in his English class who always seemed to brighten up a room when she entered.

Scotty seemed to be a pro at formulating an escape plan, always looking for a way to get out, escape, avoid.

CiCi hangs out here? he remembered thinking to himself, suddenly finding the decision to hang around much more exciting. *Free food and CiCi?* The choice was suddenly a no-brainer. There was something about CiCi's long brown hair and freckles that drew Scotty in. And the way her shirt peeked up and showed just a tiny part of her stomach was a plus. She was one of those pretty girls at school who didn't even know how beautiful she was. She was kind to people, always asking others to sit with her at lunch or offering to help someone study after school. He wasn't sure why a girl like her would be in a place like this; he assumed she lived in one of the local gated communities and went home to parents who loved her and asked her about her day. He walked in behind her, but not too close, and followed her into a brightly colored lounge area. There were guys playing cards on a side table and a couple of girls doing their homework. Some kids from school were playing basketball outside.

He lost track of CiCi when an energetic man came barreling toward him.

"Hi! I'm Andrew, but you can call me Drew," he said, and stretched his hand out with a smile. Scotty held out his hand in a pathetic attempt at a handshake, and Drew took it forcefully. He shook it hard enough to make Scotty's whole torso shake.

"People can tell a lot about you by your handshake. Make sure it's strong. And look me in the eye. Try it again," Drew said, releasing Scotty's hand. Scotty rolled his eyes. He was not in the mood for Jolly Mr. Rogers over here, and now he had lost CiCi. He humored the guy and gave a half-decent handshake, and was relieved that Drew took it as acceptable.

"Come on in, did you eat yet? There's a game of cards going on over there. You got homework?" Drew asked in rapid fire. Scotty shook his head.

"No worries. Make yourself comfortable. Let me know if you need anything." Drew patted Scotty on the back and walked toward the guys playing cards. He motioned over to Scotty and said a few words, then walked away.

As Scotty walked by the card table, someone called out. "Hey. You know how to play blackjack?" a greasy-haired blond asked. Scotty nodded. The kid patted the empty seat next to him, and Scotty sat down.

Next to Scotty was a chubby kid with red hair, who was next to a skinny Asian kid with glasses, and on the other side of the greasy-haired kid was a black kid with a lazy eye. Scotty picked up his cards; he was so thankful to have a full stomach, to see CiCi, and to not be at home. He wasn't sure if he fit in with these guys, but it was better than dealing with his dad.

Everyone looked different and talked differently, but it seemed like they all got along just fine.

"Ay, boss." A veteran AC tech's husky voice brought Scotty back to the present time.

"Hey man. Morning. How are ya?" Scotty asked, standing up to shake the tech's hand.

"Good, good. Got the coffee started," he said with a smile. The old guy's teeth were evidence of his obsessive coffee consumption, but being addicted to coffee was better than what he used to be addicted to, so Scotty left him alone.

Everyone looked different and talked differently, but it seemed like they all got along just fine.

The other guys trickled into the office, all standing around in their dirty jeans and sipping their coffee by 8 a.m.

"Okay, guys. Good morning. We've got a busy day, so let's get this going," Scotty said, sipping his coffee.

"First, the Sacred Six," Scotty instructed. The entire office erupted in sound, strong voices reciting each core principle in unison.

"Sharks never stop moving forward. Sharks never look down, always up. Sharks are always curious and learning.

Sharks always respect their environment and recognize other sharks. Sharks are always flexible. Sharks always elevate their suckerfish to new levels."

As they said each one, Scotty watched their faces. They were not just reciting a string of words. They were quoting each fundamental principle with purpose. As they went down the list, Scotty could create a clear picture in his head of each lesson and what Drew had done to help him learn each one.

Scotty ended the chant the way he always did, and the way Drew had always done. "When we live in harmony with the Sacred Six, we are truly swimming like sharks. Sharks just don't swim, they SWIM."

"Now, Goals and Gonnas. Who's first?" he asked, looking around. This was another one of Drew's traditions that Scotty carried on. Every meeting always started with the Sacred Six, then everyone listed a goal for their day and how they were going to accomplish it. Not every meeting ended the same way, but the guys insisted that it always start the same exact way. The Sacred Six was like their very own Pledge of Allegiance.

"I'll go," said a voice from the back. "My goal is to finish the Smith unit before noon."

"How ya gonna do it?" the entire team boomed in unison.

"I'm gonna clean the condenser fan and oil the fan motor."

"Very good, next?" Scotty asked.

"My g-g-goal is to learn h-h-how to use the vacuum pump," stuttered someone up front.

"How ya gonna do it?" they all asked again.

"Would someone m-m-mind showing me again h-h-how to work it? Maybe on our lunch break?" the man stuttered, looking around. Tracey lifted her chipped coffee mug as a toast and nodded.

The Goals and Gonnas practice allowed each tech to vocalize their goals and made everyone aware of everyone else's goals.

This way, they could hold each other accountable and help each other out.

"Any issues, problems, achievements, good news, or concerns we need to address before we start our day?" Scotty asked

"I got my two-year chip," Tracey said quietly from the back. She held the shiny medallion up with a timid smile like she had just won the Heisman Trophy. The entire office erupted in applause.

They could hold each other accountable and help each other out.

"Way to go, Trace!" Scotty said with a proud smile. Pregnant and homeless at 15, Tracey hadn't had it easy. After the adoption of her little boy had become final, she had found herself scared and alone and had turned to booze to fill the void. After countless stints in the ER for alcohol poisoning and two DUIs when she was 18, Tracey had found herself with a handful of pills and no hope. Scotty was the one who had found her unconscious on the park bench, called 911, and waited in the lobby for four hours as they pumped her stomach. It was Scotty who had been there when she was discharged, who had taken her home and given her some of CiCi's clothes to wear. It was Scotty who had let her recover in his beautiful guest room, and it was Scotty who had given her the ultimatum: you either stay here and go to AA, or you leave. That was two years ago, and not only was she now two years sober, but she had her own apartment, was a phenomenal AC tech, and was working on her GED.

The lights and radio in the office came on at full blast, the official start of the workday. Tools buzzed, phones rang, and 10 AC trucks with ferocious sharks splattered on them left the store in waves, off to cool down the homes of South Florida, one AC at a time.

Scotty and CiCi ate greasy pizza off paper plates and clinked their beer bottles together. They sat at their outside bar overlooking the pool, with Lionel Richie music playing softly in the background. Scotty looked over the pool and into the Intracoastal that ran behind their home. His boat was tied to the dock, bobbing in the water. His upcoming fishing trip made him regret not taking his own boat out more often, and he made a silent vow to take CiCi out on a romantic sunset ride soon. She loved boat rides, and she loved Lionel Richie!

"I was telling my kids about the shark today," CiCi smiled, biting into her pizza. "They didn't quite get it. They were asking me how they could be sharks if they weren't allowed to swim without their Mommy and Daddy," she laughed.

"Valid point," Scotty smiled. "Maybe five is too young to understand the complexities of the shark and the Sacred Six?" he asked sarcastically.

"Maybe. We'll wait 'til they're more mature. Like seven."

"Yeah. Seven's good."

As they sat in silence and watched the huge yachts pass by, their daily reminder of how good life had become, Scotty spoke.

"Ya know, I didn't think I'd be nervous or anxious about this fishing trip, but I am," Scotty said, suddenly unable to finish his pizza. "It's like when I talked to Paul, all of sudden I felt like I was seventeen all over again, feeling small. Trying to keep up with school hero Paul. I felt nervous again and remembered being in his shadow. Insecure, I guess." Scotty felt embarrassed saying it out loud. CiCi gently touched his arm.

"You aren't seventeen anymore," she said softly. "You are a very successful, kind, strong, giving, hardworking man who loves his family and loves others. You have built an incredible life for us, and you have come so far. You are not your past mistakes, and you cannot compare yourself to anyone else," she said with confidence. "What do we tell Brittany all the time?" she asked.

> "You are not your past mistakes, and you cannot compare yourself to anyone else."

"You are who you hang out with," Scotty said begrudgingly.

"Right. And who do you hang out with? Good people from rough pasts who are transforming their lives. You hang out with givers and dreamers. You've built a company that is not only wildly successful in our community but has given life back to so many people. You've given us this beautiful home and these wonderful experiences. So many families struggle to send their kids to college, especially the ones like Brittany's, and your hard work means she gets to go follow her dreams and not graduate with debt. That is life changing. You're the best person I know, and you have zero reasons to feel insecure or anxious about this trip," she said as she squeezed his arm. "You took Drew's business to the next level and grew it into a South Florida empire."

> "You are who you hang out with."

Scotty smiled at her. She was always so passionate, reassuring, and positive. CiCi was his own personal motivational speaker, and he knew she meant every word. He just didn't know if he believed in himself as much as she did. Scotty was occasionally haunted by his past and sometimes struggled with his own success. Thinking about being with Paul Gray again, after all these years, made Scotty feel like an insecure, pimply, invisible teenager who could never measure up. He thought he had outgrown these emotions—how could one phone call bring them all back?

> Scotty was occasionally haunted by his past and sometimes struggled with his own success.

"I can tell you don't completely believe me yet, but you will," CiCi said, interrupting his thoughts. She had sat up in her lounger and was looking right at him.

"No, I do, I do. It's just that he comes from this perfect family and has done all these perfect things and has been successful and here I am, an awkward kid with a dead mom and alcoholic dad and a mugshot," Scotty moaned.

"Look at me," CiCi said in all seriousness. She grabbed his chin and yanked it, so he was looking right into her eyes. He noticed those freckles and smiled. "You are not that kid anymore. Your past does not define you. Your childhood trauma does not get to steal one more second of your life. You are successful, you are smart, you are good enough and," she said as she put both hands on the side of his face, "you're really hot, too," and leaned in to kiss him. Scotty needed these pep talks occasionally, as his past always tried to hunt him down like a stalker.

> "Your past does not define you."

The morning of the fishing trip, Scotty was still anxious. He tried to remember all the things CiCi had said the night before and repeated them over and over in his head. *I'm not that seventeen-year-old kid anymore,* Scotty reminded himself as he poured his steaming hot coffee into his thermos. *I'm a grown man, and the insecurities and self-doubt are gone. I always look up, and I never look down. This'll be fun,* he thought, as he entered the garage to collect his fishing gear.

"Hey, Dad!" Brittany said, startling Scotty as he rummaged through the garage.

"Oh hey, Britty, just getting some stuff ready for the trip. You ready?"

"Yep! Who is this guy again?" she asked.

"Old buddy from high school. We kinda drifted apart when I got involved in all of my nonsense, haven't really talked to him since. Dangit, where is the . . ." Scotty trailed off.

"And he just randomly wants to hang out now?" Brittany asked, confused. Scotty realized it was pretty random, but kept pushing forward.

"Yeah, he's in town. He bought a boat from the marina down the street, so we'll take it out and—ah! Here it is!" he said, holding up a tackle box. "We'll take the boat out, spend the day on the water, catch some fish. Should be fun. Ready?" Scotty asked, fumbling with his coffee and all of the fishing gear. Brittany grabbed the tackle box and turned to go back into the house, noticing that her dad wasn't quite himself. The sun wasn't even up as they loaded everything into Scotty's truck and pulled out of the driveway. "Fishing with Paul Gray," Scotty whispered to himself.

Scotty could see Paul, and his new boat, the moment they pulled into the parking lot of the marina. The sun was just peeking up over the water, and the water was calm. Paul was hard to miss in his freshly pressed khakis and a polo shirt. What was harder to miss was the massive vessel under him, a stunning boat with a sprawling deck, spacious stern cockpit, and extra seating toward the bow of a boat.

Scotty and Brittany were walking toward the boat when Paul spotted them. He leaped onto the deck and embraced Scotty in a full-on bear hug. It caught Scotty off guard but helped to relieve some tension he had about the trip. As Paul released him from his embrace, Scotty stepped back to take a look at the older version of Paul Gray.

Scotty wondered if Paul knew they were going on a fishing trip or if maybe he thought they were going golfing at a country club. The polo shirt, perfectly pressed, had the collar flipped up, and it was hard to miss the bulge of muscle peeking out from each of the sleeves. His khakis looked brand new. His Docksiders were shining in the sunlight, and the diamonds around his wristwatch caught the small rays of sunshine coming up over the water. Paul's hair was thick and curly and he still had a full head of it, causing Scotty to subconsciously think about his own hair, wondering if Paul could see the gray popping through or the thinning area Scotty was sure would become a bald spot any day. When he smiled, Scotty immediately thought Paul would be a perfect candidate for an "after" picture in any dentist's office, although Paul had never needed braces. His teeth had always been nice, but now they perfectly straight and perfectly white. Almost too perfect. Scotty ran his tongue over his teeth and made a mental note to get to the dentist and to find his old retainer; he hoped it would still fit. He immediately regretted his wardrobe choice for today's adventure: the jean shorts Brittany always referred to as Dad shorts, a faded "I Survived the 5th Annual Dunn's Run" T-shirt, and the used-to-be-white, almost-green tennis shoes he used to mow the lawn. Scotty secretly hoped Brittany wasn't embarrassed by her fashion-challenged dad and his lack of biceps or enlarged gut from drinking beer and watching football.

Paul welcomed the two on board, clearly pleased with his new toy.

"Beautiful boat, Paul, really," Scotty said, placing his fishing gear down.

"Fell in love with her the minute I saw her. Happens a lot with me, ya know." Paul winked at Scotty and nudged him with his elbow. A handsome young man sat in the corner of the boat, eyes and thumbs fixed to his phone, in shape, looking exactly like Paul Junior minus the flipped collar.

"Scotty, this is my son, Zach. Zach, come say hello!" Paul said. Zach looked up from his phone with a quick but forced smile. "Hey," he responded, before quickly returning to the comfort and solace that only his phone could give.

"Kids and their phones, right?" Paul responded, walking toward the back of the boat. Scotty and Brittany followed.

"Paul, this is my daughter, Brittany," Scotty said, putting his hand on his daughter's back. Paul got comfortable in his captain's seat and adjusted his hat.

"Oh, right right, hi, Brittany, nice to meet you," Paul said, quickly standing up and holding out his hand to shake hers. "You jokesters ready to go?" he asked, turning the key of the boat to start the engine. He expertly navigated the giant boat out of the marina and into the Intracoastal. He cruised right by the Finn estate, but Scotty didn't even care to point it out. "Gonna name her Paula," Paul said to no one in particular, tapping the side of the boat.

"So tell me about my dad as a kid," Brittany asked Paul, with a curious but slightly mischievous smile. Scotty felt nauseous, but not because he was seasick. Brittany knew about his rough past, but he wasn't sure what stories Paul would decide to tell.

"Aww, man, Scotty was my buddy. We met in seventh-grade PE class when I accidentally decked him in the head with a kickball," Paul started, using air quotes for the word *accidentally*.

"Kid was bleeding, nose and mouth all covered in blood. I picked him up and ran him to the nurse's station. He weighed, like, nothing. So we got him all taken care of, and then we were just buddies after that. All through middle school. We went fishing together, explored the woods behind his house, dominated in neighborhood games of Cops and Robbers. Then we got to high school and we both joined the swim team."

"Wait, wait, wait. You can't just jump to high school. What about middle school? What about our fishing business?" Scotty asked.

Paul started laughing. "I totally forgot about that, man! Yes, what was it called? For Real Fishing?"

"For Real Fishing," Scotty said in his best commercial announcer voice.

"Where we catch your fish for real."

"Creative," Brittany said sarcastically. Scotty explained the premise of the business: For Real Fishing was designed to catch fish for people who didn't have time to go fishing. The business model was simple: the boys would take their hand-me-down fishing gear down after school or on the weekends and catch fish for their "clients." As an added bonus, the boys offered to place the fish on the client's pole so the client could tell their wives that they caught the fish "for real." They would go to great lengths to eliminate any evidence that 12-year-olds did the fishing, in the hope that they could deceive neighborhood wives into thinking their husbands were great fishermen.

"Did anyone use this suspect business, for real?" Brittany asked through her smile.

"Yeah, the one nice guy down the street. That guy loved our idea. And he made us feel like we were on a secret mission and that if his wife ever found out that he wasn't catching these fish 'for real,' she would be so mad. Now that I think about it, we were the probably the only two who thought it was a good idea," Paul chuckled.

"We were like fishing ninjas. We'd catch some fish and then sneak on to his back porch and attach the fish to the hook that just happened to be propped up in the corner of the back patio. We'd grab the wadded-up dollar bills he left for us in the planter—a secret stash, of course—and run home as fast as we could. He'd wink at us when he saw us around town. We felt unstoppable," Scotty explained.

"We were always doing stuff like that. When Scotty's parents were too—" Paul stopped short. "Scotty would spend the night at our house a lot. We'd stay up all night playing video games and watching movies. He'd go to church with us on Sundays, and sometimes we would even take him to school on Monday. We were like brothers," Paul said as he put his arm around Scotty's shoulder. "We would be together every day in the summer."

The two swapped stories as the boat cut through the waves. They swapped tales of middle-school adventures and sleepovers. They even tried to re-create their secret handshake. They thought back to weekends out on Mr. Gray's boat, camping in the backyard (and not making it past 11 p.m.). It was the summer between eighth grade and high school that the boys discovered their love for the water. They had spent all day swimming in the summer, jumping and racing each other in the lake just outside of Lake City, Florida, where Paul's grandparents lived. They were both determined to make the high school swim team their freshman year. Swimming in the lake was much safer than the ocean back home but much more exciting than a pool.

"Scotty and I had this little competition going on, the four hundred meter medley—remember, Scotty? He'd always try to beat my time. He was good, though, had a killer butterfly stroke.

Best butterfly on the team for sure. But then he started hanging out with the Jameson brothers and kind of . . ." Paul drifted off, suddenly realizing he may have said too much in front of Brittany.

"Yeah, after my mom died I got caught up with the wrong crowd. Hung out with the wrong people. My grades started slipping, so I got kicked off the swim team. Swim was my life, so when I lost that, I felt hopeless. Kind of stopped showing up at school altogether," Scotty said, but he knew Brittany knew this already. "I felt lost, was looking to attach to anything and anyone who made me feel seen. Got in some trouble, really was heading down the wrong path."

"You are who you hang out with," Brittany commented, repeating the phrase he and CiCi often used as she was making friends throughout school. Scotty knew the impact that words can have on someone's life, and he and Cici were intentional about being very careful about what they said around Brittany. They wanted her to hear positivity and strength. They wanted her to hear them say good things about her and about other people. Scotty could remember many of his father's catchphrases, most of which included the "F" word. Scotty knew firsthand how the things your parents say to and about you can stick with you for a lifetime. The Sacred Six was something Drew repeated and reinforced on a daily basis, and it had stuck with Scotty ever since. Scotty knew there was truth in what Drew used to say—that when you hear something enough, you begin to believe it.

> Scotty knew the impact that words can have on someone's life. . . . When you hear something enough, you begin to believe it.

"Right. That's something we would tell Britty even as a little girl, and it stuck. Kids are listening, always listening, which is why as parents we have to be so careful about what we say and how we say it. You know what I mean, Paul?" Scotty asked, pretty sure Paul didn't. Paul nodded, and seemed eager to dive right back into narrating one of Scotty's most regrettable life choices.

"And those jerks didn't even vouch for you," Paul continued with his story. "Ran off and let you take the fall. I couldn't believe it when I heard you were up at 44th Street. I was like, 'little' Scotty? Doing time?' I couldn't believe it!" Paul said with a chuckle.

Out of the corner of his eye, Scotty saw Brittany's mouth drop to the floor. This part, she didn't know. Until now. He avoided eye contact with her and tried to push through the story.

"Yep. Possession of an illegal substance—one hundred and eighty days. It was just a few weeks after I turned eighteen. Cops pulled us over for a broken taillight and asked to search the car. Of course, we were freaking out, but when the cops found what they found, the guys acted like they had never seen weed before. But it was my car so I took the fall for them, and since it was my first real offense, they gave me a little break. Didn't have to do all one hundred and eighty days, but it was the worst two months of my life. But thank God, I got it together and was able to get back on track," Scotty said, realizing how fast he was talking, a result of nerves and wanting to get through the story as quickly as possible. Finally, he looked over at Brittany, who looked like a deer in headlights. "Enough about me. Let's talk about Mr. All-American over here," Scotty said, playfully shoving Paul with his shoulder.

"This guy, he was a beast," Scotty started.

"Was?" Paul interjected, flexing his muscles. "Ask my personal trainer, he'll tell you that I am still a beast." Paul smirked. Brittany tried not to roll her eyes.

"He was captain of the football team and swim team in high school, did barely any campaigning and won Student Government president by a landslide," Scotty said.

"My competition never stood a chance, can't even remember that nerd's name," Paul said proudly.

Brittany, spunky like her mom, couldn't help it this time and her eyes almost rolled out of her head. Scotty knew he was losing Brittany fast and the day had just begun.

"Prom king, too?" Scotty asked, even though he knew the answer. Paul nodded with pride.

"While we were all frantic about filling out applications for college, schools were coming to school to find this guy. Where'd you end up going?" Scotty asked.

"Got my undergraduate in business at USC and my master's at the University of Chicago. Started as an intern at the place I'm at now, cutthroat, I tell ya. Had to hurt some feelings to get to the top, but that's business." Paul shrugged.

"People 'round Chicago know me, Scotty. They either love me or they hate me. Made some enemies to get where I am, but I gotta look out for me, you know? They know not to mess with Paul Gray. They know I mean business and I'm not afraid to call people out, ya know what I mean? People who love me love me, people who hate me are just mad 'cause they ain't got what I got. Now I'm VP of sales, and with bonuses I'm making 'bout a mil. Not bad for an all-American kid from Broward, huh?" Paul bragged as he nudged Scotty.

"I'm busy, but I'm living and loving the snowbird life, too. I love popping down here for a break from the Chicago wind," Paul said as he propped his feet up on the steering wheel and laced his fingers behind his head. "I mean the tax man thinks I snowbird, but who really snowbirds?" Paul winked and a mischievous smile spread across his face. "It's all good, everyone lies about that stuff," he said, explaining himself even though nobody had questioned him about it. It was silent for a while as the boat roared into the open ocean, quiet except for the clicks and beeps of Zach's phone.

Scotty peered out into the water, Paul's sentence about how much he made replaying in his head. He was trying not to let the realization that he made more money than Paul—a lot more money than Paul—get to his head. He couldn't help but feel a tiny sense of satisfaction, knowing full well that Paul only shared this information because he was confident it would impress Scotty. Scotty had a hard time processing the information. He felt proud, but then he felt guilty for feeling proud. Scotty's inner cheerleader was doing backflips in his head. *How could the second-chances AC guy be making more than the all-American VP? And what did it mean? Did it even matter? What did it change about their dynamic?* Scotty tried to let it go. *Don't make it a big deal,* he thought to himself, *stop thinking about it. Let this be a lesson not to make assumptions.* Scotty felt a small private victory and grew a little more confident, but Paul still didn't have a clue.

"So tell me about your wife," Scotty said after a few minutes of silence and after the cheering in his head stopped.

"Ah, Charlotte. Real trophy I got there. Gorgeous girl, smart, funny, life of the party. Met her at a networking event a few years ago. Hottest girl in the whole place and she came right over to me," Paul smiled. "She walked right up to me and said she had heard things about me, and she liked a powerful man. We hit it off right away."

"What does she do?" Brittany asked, now clearly unimpressed with anything Paul had to say.

"She stays home. She had a dead-end job at an accounting firm, but I told her to quit, let me take care of her. She loves to travel, so we're always in new places. We're going to Rome next month for our third anniversary."

"Third?" Scotty asked.

"Oh yeah, she's my second wife. She was the upgrade," he winked. Scotty didn't respond and was suddenly uncomfortable about how Paul was talking about women in front of his daughter.

"Me and Junie, you remember June? Senior year?"

"Yeah, yeah, yeah!" Scotty replied, remembering the gorgeous cheerleader who had tagged along with Paul throughout high school.

"She ended up going to USC right along with me. Didn't trust me a million miles away on a college campus without her, so she came along. Can't blame her," Paul smiled.

"So we did the college thing, she survived all my college shenanigans and then she was all expecting to get married, so I got her this crazy rock, took her out to dinner, and asked her to marry me. I think we got pregnant with Zach that night."

"Gross," Zach said, his second word since the boat left.

"I mean any woman who could put up with me through college is a keeper, right? She was loyal, just like a puppy. We tried to make it work, but I was out and about too much. And she was always complaining about spending money and debt and all of that nonsense. I kept tellin' her that we can't just try to keep up with the Joneses, we gotta *be* the Joneses, right? She would have never let me get this boat, would have said, 'We've got too much debt. We don't need it,' in that whiny voice. But I wanted to travel and buy new cars and go to the casino and she was just such a buzzkill, man. Then you add my late nights, traveling, networking events. Didn't work out. So we got divorced about four years ago." Scotty did the math.

"Mmm-hmm," he acknowledged.

"And now Charlotte and I are living the dream. You'll have to meet her, she's a ten and doesn't ask too many questions, you know?" Paul smiled, giving Scotty a thumbs-up. Brittany pretended to gag.

Scotty waited for Paul to ask him about CiCi, but he didn't, of course.

"That's great, man, yeah, I'd love to meet her. And you need to meet CiCi."

"CiCi Peters?"

"Well, CiCi Finn now, but yeah," Scotty said proudly.

"Scotty Finn snagged CiCi Peters? Way to go, man!" Paul raised his hand to high-five Scotty. Scotty wasn't crazy about the term *snagged* but humored Paul and high-fived him anyway.

"When I finally got out of jail, I had nobody to call. The only number I had was the number to the Boys and Girls Club, which I got from the judge with strict instructions. I had no friends, my mom was gone, my dad was unstable. All I had was the Boys and Girls Club to help me pick up the pieces. That's how I met Drew. When I got first got to the club I knew I had no choice but to make it work. I knew it was a second chance. God always gives us second chances. But I thank my lucky stars every day for the Boys and Girls Club that led me to Drew, who led me to CiCi."

> "God always gives us second chances."

"He was a good guy, Drew was," Scotty smiled. "Really stepped in to be the dad I needed around that time. He let me work for him at his shop and CiCi and I got to know each other better away from school. We dated for about three years, and I proposed by the lighthouse on the beach. We got married and had Brittany soon after." Scotty smiled, winking at Brittany and trying to curb her annoyance.

"Sounds nice man. Happy for you. And you like what you're doing? Fixing ACs?" Paul asked. Scotty knew that ever since he had gone to jail, Paul had started to pity him. Maybe it had started before that, all of those nights Scotty's parents had been too drunk to pick him up from swim team and Paul's parents had brought him home. Or maybe it was when Scotty's mom died. Whenever it was, Scotty knew Paul felt sorry for him, the kid who could never quite measure up and fell into trouble. Part of Scotty knew that Paul still felt that way, even now. The way he had asked if he was happy fixing ACs felt condescending and almost accusatory.

"I think this is good," Paul said, shutting off the engine and bringing the boat to a stop. The water was calm and Scotty got to work preparing the fishing gear. Brittany jumped up to help, handing Scotty what he needed and portioning out the bait.

"You going to fish, Zach?" Scotty called toward the center console, where Zach sat still, mindlessly scrolling through his phone.

"Nah, I'm good," he said without looking up. Scotty glanced at Paul, who just shrugged.

"What are you going to school for?" Paul asked Brittany.

She baited her line and threw it overboard, fighting through her annoyance before answering. "Business," she replied. Scotty could tell Brittany was not Paul's biggest fan, and smiled to himself at how much she was like CiCi.

"Ah. Smart girl. Want some advice?" he asked, but continued before she could answer.

"Few things: you gotta get yours. Nobody is going to be watching your back, nobody is going to hold your hand. You want something, you go get it. Now people aren't gonna like you for that. They're gonna be mad that you got what they want, but that's life. Another thing: don't trust people. You think they're your friends and *bam*! They throw you under the bus and take the promotion that you were after. But ya know what, they'll get theirs. You rise up, become their boss, then fire them for some BS to show 'em who's in charge." Paul laughed, clearly speaking from experience.

"And a third thing: you don't need anyone else. You have everything you need to be successful; you don't need the approval or help of anyone else. Everything should be on your terms, so if you fail, it's on you, but if you succeed, it's all on you. All these self-help fuddy-duddies can tell you that business is about people, but it ain't true. Business is about the bottom line, the profit. If you can't make your people make those goals and make that money, you're not a good leader and you're not gonna be successful. You're not a real businessman, or businesswoman in your case, if people aren't afraid to piss you off. If they know you'll come for them, they'll do their job and you'll make money. We're not here to hold hands and sing kumbaya. We're here to get a job done, and anyone that can't handle it can go. We all need to do what we gotta do. That's my two cents."

Brittany couldn't even breathe, let alone respond. All of it was so completely the polar opposite of everything she knew to be true. She kept her back toward Paul, speechless and annoyed. She pretended to be focused on fishing, and Paul didn't seem to notice her lack of response.

Scotty could let a lot of things go. The way Paul talked about his wife, the way Paul bragged about his questionable business practices—but one thing he couldn't let slide was someone telling his daughter that business is about profit before people. He knew Brittany could handle herself. He knew, at least he hoped she knew, that everything Paul had spouted out was the opposite of everything she knew to be true. But what kind of dad would he be if he just let someone speak to her about her future career that way?

"Actually—" Scotty began, finally reaching the point where he couldn't let Paul's comments go. But just as he opened up his mouth, he was interrupted.

"Holy hell. Do y'all see that?" Paul yelled. Everyone followed the direction of his pointed finger, directed into the water toward the horizon.

"What? What is it?" Brittany asked, with a little apprehension in her voice. Paul was quiet. Focused.

"What?" Scotty asked. At that moment, a slice of gray penetrated the water and moved slowly forward, perpendicular to the boat. It took Scotty a second to realize what it was.

"Is that a—" Scotty started

"It sure as hell is, Scotty boy. That right there is a shark. Right there! I saw one last time I came up here, too! What a sight!"

"Should we bring our lines in or anything? I don't want him to come near the boat," Brittany said, sounding a little more anxious this time. The shark disappeared and then reappeared a few feet closer to the boat. Scotty could see an aha moment in Paul's face as he made a beeline for the back of the boat. He opened up a large storage container and pulled out a huge blue bucket and a heavy-duty fishing line.

"This'll do it," Paul said quietly as he pushed by Brittany.

"This'll do what?" she asked nervously. "What are you doing?"

Without a word, Paul emptied the bucket of bloody fish off the side of the boat.

"What in the world?" Brittany shrieked, looking over at Scotty in desperation. Scotty was nervous again but didn't want to overreact. Paul seemed experienced and like he knew what he was doing. And it was his boat.

"It's a baby. With this rod and that chum, we might just be able to get him on board!"

"Is that even legal?" Brittany shrieked.

"Eh, we're not going to keep the guy. Just bring him up to say hello. Scotty, grab that net over there for me, will ya, buddy?" Paul asked, pointing to the back of the boat. Scotty hesitated and glanced at Brittany, who looked dumbfounded that he was even considering it, then hurried to grab the net.

Scotty saw that the shark was quickly approaching the dead fish that was floating near the boat. The thing had to be few feet long, and even from a distance Scotty could see the telltale markings of the ocean predator. Paul threw his line in and steadied himself. He was focused and determined to do this, and nobody was going to tell him otherwise.

Scotty recognized Paul's focused expression; it was the same one he'd had as he stood on the diving platform in high school, determined to cut through the water like a knife and leave everyone else in his wake.

"Here we go!" Paul shouted as the line tightened. "Got 'm on my line!" Scotty and Brittany stood back, watching the young shark fight and flail in the water. They watched as Paul pulled and reeled, pulled and reeled, making progress with each tug. The shark inched its way toward the edge of the boat, splashing and slapping its tail on the water. The shark was getting tired, and Paul was gaining strength. The two battled for what felt like hours, each determined to win, Paul's muscles swelling like he had just left the gym. *His personal trainer must be proud,* Scotty thought.

"I'm gonna pull him up! Back away!" Paul shouted as the tired young shark got closer to the boat. Brittany and Scotty stood in silence. Their whole life was influenced by this misunderstood and dynamic fish. Paul was focused and oblivious all at the same time. The moment so intense that even Zach put down his phone.

2

Shark Tales

Scotty snapped to his senses and into action. As Paul tugged and pulled, Scotty moved toward him and looked over the side of the boat. The shark was thrashing, but the fight had worn him out. Scotty wasn't sure what Paul's plan was, but he knew it was illegal to bring a shark onto the boat. He put his hand on Paul's back.

"Hey, Brittany, look at this. We can't pull it up, it's illegal, but you can come look at it right here on the side of the boat," Scotty called out, half to Brittany and half to Paul in a passive-aggressive way to let him know that they wouldn't be bringing the shark on board. Brittany and Zach came to the edge of the boat and looked over the side. The gray and white predator was just a baby shark a few feet long, and Scotty could look right into its glossy, black eyes. Paul's muscles relaxed, and he exhaled. Both he and the shark were exhausted from the fight.

"I can't believe the line didn't break," Scotty said. Paul beamed with pride. "Only skill, Scotty my boy, only skill can do that," he said proudly.

Paul caught his breath. "Ya know, I've always thought of myself as a kind of shark. In the business world, ya know," he said, sitting back on the padded seat, the shark bobbing right under the surface of the water. "They're the top predator, right? I mean, everyone knows not to mess with a shark. Even you, Scotty, you're afraid to bring him up here because you know what he's capable of. It's a respect thing, a fear thing. People hate sharks, but sharks don't care. They're not out there to make friends; they're out there to chomp the hell out of anyone who gets in their way. It's how you get things done," Paul said, clearly proud of his analogy. Brittany shot Scotty an annoyed look, almost begging him to throw Paul overboard.

"Zach, Brittany, get your phones so we can take a picture. Then we'll unhook him and let him go," Scotty instructed. The group stood awkwardly by the edge of the boat and tried to squeeze together to get the shot. Scotty grabbed a pair of wire cutters and inched toward the hook. The sharp teeth made Scotty's stomach drop, but he was determined to get this shark back into the deep. He looked directly into the shark's eyes and realized they almost looked like they were pleading with him. He gave the line a snap, and after a few moments the shark darted into the water.

"Ya know, Drew taught me a lot about sharks during the time I worked for him."

"The AC guy taught you about sharks?" Paul asked a little doubtfully, still catching his breath.

"Absolutely! Yeah. I am who I am because of what Drew taught me about sharks and the Sacred Six."

"I don't know, Scotty boy. I mean, I've owned a few boats and have been out on more chartered fishing trips than I can remember. I've fished all over the world and I have actually brought sharks on board. I've been to Asia on business trips and have eaten shark fin soup, Scotty. No offense, but I seriously doubt your buddy the AC tech would know anything about sharks that I don't already know and what the heck is a Sacred Six?"

"You know what?" Brittany boomed, stopping Paul midsentence. Scotty whirled around to look at Brittany, surprised not only at her volume but the fact that she had interrupted Paul at all.

"Drew was not just 'some AC tech,' okay? He was my grandfather, and he was one of the most selfless and successful men I've ever known. The lessons he taught my dad molded him into the man he is today," Brittany said, trying to control the shakiness of her voice. Scotty gently put his hand on her arm.

"He has a good wife and family because of what Drew taught him. And you're not the only successful businessman on this boat, ya know? You could learn a thing or two or six from this AC tech over here," she said, her voice trembling, clearly upset by both Paul's arrogance and her dad's timidness. He gently squeezed her arm. "You're so proud of your boat? We've got a boat, too. Big deal. Bigger than this, but you don't hear us boasting about it," she continued.

"Okay, Britty, that's enough," Scotty said softly.

"You make a million dollars a year? Whoop-dee-doo, you're so full of yourself. You're not the only successful person on this boat. Maybe take five seconds to actually listen and care about other peo—"

"Enough," Scotty said, more firmly this time. Scotty looked at Paul, over at Zach, back to Brittany, and then back to Paul. Everyone on the boat was uncomfortable and silent, the energy changing. Brittany shook her arm from Scotty's grasp and headed toward the rear of the boat.

Paul looked shocked and confused, and crossed his arms and thought to himself: *Man, Scotty's a wimp, can't even control his daughter and her attitude. Men should be alpha dogs. I'd never tolerate that in my house. Same ol' Scotty, living in dysfunction and chaos. And an AC tech is not a successful businessman. Poor kid, she is lost and clueless about what success really is. No way Scotty has a boat nicer than mine, he doesn't even have a degree. No way,* Paul thought.

Scotty could tell Brittany's comments got Paul thinking. He stood there with his arms crossed, looking contemplative. Scotty followed Brittany.

"Hey, Britty, you okay?" he asked, sitting down next to her. She rolled her eyes and Scotty smiled slightly, realizing how much she reminded him of CiC when she was fired up.

"Yeah. I mean no, but it's fine. It's whatever. I'm just so tired of him talking about himself and his ego and talking down to you like you're some nobody. Like Grandy was a nobody," she said, looking away. Brittany was rubbing her shark tooth that hung around her neck on a chain, something she did when she was upset.

"I know. It's okay. I'm sorry that you felt uncomfortable. I will talk to him, okay?" he assured her.

"Yeah, whatever," she said dismissively. Scotty got back up and moved toward Paul with purpose.

"She okay?" Paul asked with a smile.

"She's okay. She loved Drew a lot. And she's just like her mom; she speaks her mind," he said unapologetically.

Paul nodded, but thought, *No, I get it! You need to get your wife and your daughter in check.*

"So what'd Drew the shark expert tell you about sharks? Did he ever catch one?" Paul asked. Scotty could sense annoyance or defensiveness in Paul's tone.

"During that time of my life, I was on the brink of addiction. I was empty and without any direction. I was doing whatever I could to fill a void in my heart. I was just floating through life with no purpose or direction. I remember the first time I hung out with Drew. He and CiCi took me home after a day at the Boys and Girls Club, which is when I put two and two together and realized that CiCi was Drew's daughter. The ride was quiet and awkward and I mumbled a quick 'thank you' as I jumped out of the truck and avoided eye contact with CiCi at all costs. When Drew dropped me off at home, I assumed that was the last time he'd ever let me within one hundred feet of his daughter, and that he would probably write me off as a waste of space, like everyone else had. Which is why I was so surprised the next morning when he showed up at my door. He told me to get dressed and meet him out in his truck in fifteen minutes. I listened. I threw on some clothes and jumped into his truck without a word," Scotty said, quickly glancing at Paul. Paul was fumbling with his fishing gear but stopped to look at Scotty when he paused, as if he was interested in hearing more. Scotty went on.

"I was just floating through life with no purpose or direction."

"We drove for a while in silence. Drew asked me if I knew why he named his company Shark's, and I shrugged and shook my head. He told me it was because he had always been fascinated with sharks, even as a kid. They are at the top of the food chain in the ocean. As he got older, he learned that if he could adopt a few characteristics of a shark, he could become a shark too and have an impact. So he created **The Sacred Six**. During our drive, he mentioned that he had seen me on that diving platform during my high school swim meets. Sometimes when he had to pick up or drop off CiCi he'd stop by the pool and watch us practice.

"He learned that if he could adopt a few characteristics of a shark, he could become a shark too and have an impact."

"He said, 'When you are a shark, you don't just swim, you SWIM. I've seen the focus in your eyes, the power in your swim. I've seen you prepare yourself before a competition. I've seen you at early morning practices and when you stay long after practice is over. The first thing you need to know about being a shark is that **sharks never stop moving forward**. They are in constant motion, or they die. If they go backward, they drown. It's called *failing forward.* If you live in the past, you'll never improve your future. The best lessons in life are the ones you pay for, Scotty. **Sharks never look down; they always look up.** Your attitude is the only thing that can stop you. Stay positive, no matter what! Sharks don't act like common fish, because they are different—they are sharks. **Sharks are curious**; they are always paying attention and are always learning.'

"Drew kept his eyes on the road the entire time he was telling me all of this, but his intensity and passion were real. I had never had a person talk to me like this before. It was a little scary, but I knew it was good for me. It felt like a lot of information to take in all at once, but I was thankful that he was investing time in me.

"If you live in the past, you'll never improve your future. The best lessons in life are the ones you pay for"

"Then—I remember it like it was yesterday—as we stopped at a red light, he turned in his seat and looked right at me and said, '**Sharks respect their environment and recognize and respect other sharks**. And I see one now, Scotty. Sharks can grow about ten to twelve inches a year; you need to grow, my man, but no doubt you are a shark.' He looked forward and I looked forward, too, taking in the moment." Scotty got goosebumps telling the story now, just as he had in that old truck when it happened, and always cited it as the moment that began his transformation into who he was today. He remembered it being the first time Drew ever said his famous catchphrase "When you are a shark, you don't just swim, you SWIM" out loud, but he didn't explain it until much later. It would become a foundational principle in Scotty's development and growth.

"In that truck that day, Drew helped me learn and recite four of the Sacred Six. Every time they rolled off my tongue, I felt a little more empowered. At Shark's AC Repair Service we start every morning meeting reciting the Sacred Six."

"Cute," Paul said, unimpressed. "If Drew was there at our practices, I wonder if he ever saw how fast I could do the butterfly?" Paul asked. Scotty recognized this behavior in Paul, his habit of always turning the attention back on himself. But Scotty knew that this time it was because he was uncomfortable and dazed and so he reverted to his narcissistic instincts.

Scotty stayed focused because he knew he had Paul's full attention, so he sat back down on the damp boat seats and continued once Paul gave him permission.

"Sharks are typically loners, right?" Scotty asked. "They aren't the ocean's most social creatures, but this does not mean they live a life of solitude. Some species of sharks work with others when they are hunting. They know they can work together to take down larger prey. They understand the strengths of other sharks and use them to achieve a common goal. A shark doesn't allow a dolphin or a starfish to help it hunt, but they will allow other sharks. They instinctively know how to identify others with a similar mindset and work ethic," Scotty said matter-of-factly, thinking about the way Drew had demonstrated this to him.

"They understand the strengths of other sharks and use them to achieve a common goal."

"Just like you can identify a shark in the water by its telltale markings, like we did, you can identify the sharks in your own life by their character, work ethic, and the way they treat other people," Scotty continued. "I now know a shark when I see one. It's not rocket science if you pay attention. Most leaders tell their people what is wrong with them, but not Drew; he influenced us because he always focused on what was right with us."

"You can identify the sharks in your own life by their character, work ethic, and the way they treat other people."

Scotty watched Paul's face for a reaction, but he was hard to read.

"As I drove with Drew that day, I had no idea where we were going literally, but I knew I had already taken a trip spiritually. I was beginning to trust someone for the first time in my life. I learned over time that Drew always knew where we were going, always had a mission and destination in mind—another trait of a shark. But back then, I just could tell he knew where we were going. We pulled into an aquarium downtown. We walked in silence through the parking lot, into the building. He paid for my ticket and I followed him as he quickly made a beeline for the shark exhibit. He pointed to a bench in front of a massive shark tank. I sat. We sat in silence for a while until something came gliding into focus. It was a shark. One by one, more sharks came into view. They swam peacefully, methodically, always aware of their surroundings.

"'Why do you think they don't go after each other?' Drew asked me. 'They're predators. They eat meat. They are surrounded by meat that can't get away. Why isn't it a bloodbath?' I remember shrugging but contemplating the question. I could see out of the corner of my eye that he was looking at me, expecting an answer. I told him I wasn't sure, but he wasn't going to let me off easy. I remember thinking about it, and then I said 'Because they're all the same?'

"You don't attack someone you respect."

"Drew looked at me, pleased. 'Is that a statement or a question?' he asked. I wasn't sure. And I wasn't sure what his point was."

Scotty looked over at Paul, surprised that Paul was still paying attention.

"'They rarely attack each other because they're all the same,'" Scotty said, speaking to Paul with purpose. "'Sharks recognize and respect other sharks, Scotty.

You don't attack someone you respect.'"

"They may not all be the same species, but they know that they are all sharks.There is enough room in there for all of them to be sharks without being a threat to each other," Scotty explained. He waited for a response from Paul, but he just nodded.

Paul pushed Zach playfully on the shoulder. "See, Zach, this is why I tell you: when others perceive you as a threat, you're in control." Zach nodded in acknowledgment. Scotty heard Brittany try to muffle a laugh from behind him.

"It's not about being a threat, though," Scotty explained, "It's about being able to identify sharks in your life and not perceiving their success, or their existence, as a threat. We have no room for haters. Sharks can identify other sharks and respect them enough to share the same space without having to kill each other," Scotty tried to explain.

"So what happened after the aquarium? You go home and hang out with CiCi?" Paul asked, giving a suggestive nod toward Scotty.

"Not quite. Drew wasn't done with his lessons about the sharks. He pointed out two more things: all the sharks were swimming forward, with direction and purpose. They didn't zig and zag through the water, and they *never* went backward. They're actually not capable of swimming backward; they would drown if they did. As sharks, we must be focused on progress and forward movement. We learn from our mistakes and work hard not to repeat them. You don't make mistakes twice, because the second time you do it, it's a choice. Once we learn a lesson we don't revert to our old ways; we don't go back to who we used to be. **Sharks never, I mean *never*, swim** backward," Scotty explained. "It was one thing to hear Drew say it in the truck, but when I saw the sharks moving myself, it all began to make sense. Everything he said in that truck, I saw at the aquarium.

> "You don't make mistakes twice, because the second time you do it, it's a choice."

"Another thing he taught me that was fascinating is that sharks are made of cartilage. All cartilage. Like this flabby part of your ear or the tip of your nose. Most other fish have skeletons made of bone. The fact that sharks are made of cartilage makes them flexible and adaptable. This is one of the most important aspects of a shark; they are flexible and can easy adapt to their surroundings," Scotty explained. Paul nodded and subtly tugged at the cartilage on his ear. "Some sharks can survive in both salt and freshwater. Cartilage is lighter than bone, so sharks can change direction swiftly and efficiently, unlike people or fish. Sometimes making a fast change or any change at all is the most difficult thing for people to do. Deep, huh?" Scotty asked. Paul looked blank but Scotty knew something was happening and trusted his instinct.

"So after our lessons were over, we left. We left the aquarium and Drew brought me home. Told me to expect him the next day, same time. Sure enough, this guy shows up at my door at 8 a.m. the next day. I hopped in his truck and what do you know, we're back at the aquarium. We walk through the parking lot, he pays for my ticket, we make a beeline for the shark exhibit. He points to the bench. I sit. This time, we don't have to wait. The sharks are circling and swimming in front of us, graceful yet terrifying at the same time. We were quiet for a while, just watching. Then Drew asked me what I noticed," Scotty said, thinking about the dark aquarium, the hard wooden bench, and the faint smell of fish.

"I shrugged again, of course, not wanting to give him the wrong answer. *What did I notice?* I remember thinking to myself. *That we are sitting in front of a tank full of sharks. Again.* But I didn't say it. I stayed quiet, hoping he'd offer up the answer. No luck. So I watched. I looked for markings on the sharks that would help me tell them apart, but they all looked pretty much the same. I looked for anything new in the tank that had been added since the day before. It was all the same. There was nothing extraordinary. They were just sharks. Drew's silent expectation for an answer started to bug me. I wasn't crazy about playing games with a guy I barely knew.

"'They're slow,' I said, aggravated. 'They're just swimming around. They're slow. What am I supposed to be looking for?' I asked, this time a little louder. I was over it. I was bored and frustrated and not understanding the point. Drew did a little half-nod.

"'Okay. They're swimming slowly. What else?' he asked me with a smile. I remember wanting to scream. *What else?! There is literally nothing else to look at!* I thought for sure this guy was nuts.

"'They're just swimming and swimming. That's it! They just keep swimming,' I said and threw my hands up. I wanted to get out of there. The curve of the thick glass and the dim lighting was giving me a headache. And his games weren't helping, either.

"'Aha!' he said, with a pointed finger in the air.

"'Aha what?' I asked, annoyed.

"'They never stop their movement. They never stop! Ever. You know why?'

"'Because they're sharks?' I replied sarcastically.

"'Because if they stop, they will die,' Drew explained. 'Most species, anyway. They need to keep moving to keep the water flowing through the gills, which allows them to breathe. Their constant movement, their relentless spirit, is a matter of life or death. **Sharks never stop swimming**,' Drew said with excitement.

"Their movement gives them life," Scotty explained to Paul. "How many people do you know who are stagnant after a mistake or just stagnant people period? You can overcome any mistake if you don't quit. Successful people aren't perfect and they make mistakes, but they keep moving and outwork everyone, too. You can overwhelm a mistake with hard work.

> "You can overcome any mistake if you don't quit."

"Drew constantly reinforced the Sacred Six. In fact, he would always say, 'Smart companies are training-and-development companies masquerading in their core business.' Shark's AC Repair Service is nothing more than a training-and-development company. That is why we are successful—we grow our people. Sharks can grow a foot a year, so we as people should, too. Every time Drew taught us a lesson, he made us repeat it out loud, and he would always reinforce it. It was annoying at first, but his lessons were like a seed that first grew in your head but didn't take root until it grew in your heart."

Paul added bait to his line and cast it out into the water. The two watched the bobber dance on the water before becoming still.

Paul turned to Scotty. "That's why Junie was such a pain, Scotty! I was always working, traveling, doing stuff, never home, never quitting. I was out there trying to be a shark and she was always holding me back. Talking about priorities and downtime and all that mess. I'm trying to 'never stop moving,' and she's over here crying because I never quit!" Paul moaned, trying desperately to relate to the story.

> "His lessons were like a seed that first grew in your head but didn't take root until it grew in your heart."

This is going to be harder than I thought, Scotty thought. It seemed like Paul was trying hard to see himself in each of the stories as a shark, but it wasn't quite connecting. What surprised Scotty the most was Paul's ability to listen to a story from another person for this length of time, so he gave him credit for that. *The Sacred Six is a movement. I'll get him... I hope. If I can crack this nut and teach Paul how to SWIM, Drew will be proud. Paul has some issues but he doesn't even know it.* Scotty thought to himself, *This guy is a piece of work.*

"Never stop moving means constantly seeking balance and progress in all areas of your life and not stopping until you reach your goals. It's not moving forward with your own agenda while leaving everyone else in your life to fend for themselves. Never stop moving means waking up every day determined to progress further than the day before, even if you're worn out or tired or the current is too strong. Sharks never stop their movement. The constant forward movement literally gives sharks life. And when you're a shark, you need progress and growth to feel alive. If your life isn't growing and improving, something is wrong. You need to go back and check yourself against the Sacred Six."

> "If your life isn't growing and improving, something is wrong."

Paul nodded, his attention on the bobber in the water. *I'm losing him,* Scotty thought, *he's over it.* Scotty gave Paul credit for listening this long and turned toward the back of the boat to check on Brittany. *I probably gave him too much, it's like drinking from a fire hose,* Scotty thought.

"So did he take you back to the aquarium again? Y'all should have bought an annual pass at this point," Paul joked, still watching the water. Surprised that Paul wanted to hear more, Scotty sat back down. *What is the next one?* Scotty thought to himself, quickly running through the Sacred Six in his head. Scotty now knew he had a big fish on the line. Could he reel him in, catch, and release Paul into the SWIM movement? Scotty knew one thing: Drew had taught him how to be a fisher of people.

"My education on sharks was just beginning, and about to get a lot more intense. Drew dropped me off at home, and told me to expect him even earlier the next day. The next day, this guy came knocking, and I jumped into his truck half asleep. We bypassed the exit for the aquarium and I noticed we were heading toward the coast. We parked in a parking lot overlooking the water. My heart started racing when I saw shark-shaped wooden signs that read *Wacky Wally's Shark Feeding Tours*.

"We walked down the boardwalk lined with little fishing boats and expensive yachts. I stopped when Drew stopped; we were in front of an older fishing boat with the words *Wacky Wally* painted on the side.

"A big scruffy black guy with his two front teeth missing came up out of nowhere and greeted Drew with a big bear hug and a 'What's up, bro?' Unfortunately for me, Drew's VIP status and personal connection with Wally meant we jumped directly onto a boat and were headed out toward the ocean before I could say 'Wacky Wally.'

"Our guide explained that their success rates for seeing sharks was about ninety percent, and showed us the big bucket of smelly chum he'd be using to bring the sharks right to the boat. Sure enough, Wacky Wally throws the dead fish off the side and here they come, their powerful bodies slicing through the water—first one, then two and three and four. I was mesmerized, but Drew brought me back to the present.

"'What do you notice?' he asked, his famous opening line. Drew was always asking questions.

"'They're hungry,' I said, as a statement this time instead of a question.

"'Right. Were these sharks right by the boat before we threw in the chum?' Drew asked me.

"'Not right by the boat. But they were out there,' I said, more confident this time.

"'Right. It's not like they just happened to be swimming by the second we dumped in the fish and just happened upon a free lunch. They were out there, planning, looking, searching. Sharks can smell a drop of blood in the ocean and they were out there...

"'Hunting,' I finished for him. Drew nodded. He explained that sharks were always looking for their next food source, their next kill. **Sharks are curious and are always learning.** They didn't get what they wanted by chance. They went after it. They were hyperfocused on their surroundings so that at the first smell of blood in the water, the first opportunity, they were tuned in. They didn't depend on the leftovers of others, or for another shark to bring them food. They knew that if they wanted it, they'd have to go get it."

Scotty explained that the real lesson was that even though they smelled blood in the water, they surveyed the environment and were curious before they attacked.

"Drew told me that sharks respect the ocean and the ocean respects them. They don't kill any- and everything; they are curious and investigate everything before they strike. 'Sharks aren't pigs, Scotty,' I remember Drew saying as we watched the sharks together, 'but they are decisive.' It was another pivotal moment for me, a moment that challenged me and caused me to rethink a lot of things about myself.

"Drew told me that sharks respect the ocean and the ocean respects them. They don't kill any-and everything; they are curious and investigate everything before they strike."

"Ya know, the biggest misconception is that sharks attack anything that swims by. In fact, sharks hate the way people taste. The way a shark investigates and learns is to smell, bump up against things, or to put something in their mouth. That's why people get shark bites; but death by shark is rare." Scotty noticed that Zach was tuned in, listening carefully. Brittany had heard this story a million times, it got her goat every time, but even she was paying attention. Scotty looked down at the shark tattoo on his calf and smiled.

"If you are brave enough, you can even swim with sharks. You see it on TV all the time. Shark experts will tell you, when sharks bite a human it's because they see this strange creature flailing in the water and they bite it just to see what it is because they are curious by nature, but they normally spit it right out—because we taste nasty to them. I've even heard crazy stories about experienced ocean swimmers punching sharks in the face and the shark leaving them alone out of respect."

Paul raised his eyebrows and Scotty was almost certain he was picturing him punching a shark in the eye and knocking it out in the water.

"After our shark feeding adventure, we went back to the shore. 'You taking your new friend in the cage?' Wally asked, smiling and shaking Drew's hand as we stepped off the boat. Drew winked at Wally and then at me. *The cage?* I thought in horror. *What is the cage?* I screamed inside. We headed back to the car. I asked him about the cage and he just smirked and said, 'You'll see.' The whole drive home I was on edge, and practically ran into the house as he pulled into the driveway. Drew rolled down the window and called out to me, 'Tomorrow's a big day. So much more to learn,' and winked as he drove off. I wanted to puke.

"When he picked me up the next morning, he threw a pair of faded swim trunks at me and smiled without looking at me. I hated how much he was enjoying this. We bypassed the exit for the aquarium and headed back to Wacky Wally's. But as we parked and walked down the dock, we simply waved to Wally and walked by him. Wally gave Drew a knowing smirk and I wanted to push both of them into the water. We followed the boardwalk to the very end until we stopped under another shark-shaped wooden sign." Scotty took a breath.

"Where'd ya go?" Zach asked, scooting closer to Scotty.

"The sign said *Crazy Carl's Shark Diving Expeditions*," Scotty said calmly, feeling nervous all over again.

"No way!" Paul shouted, playfully shoving Scotty.

"Yep. Shark diving. The boat was huge and there was—"

"Bigger than this?" Paul asked.

"Yeah, much," Scotty said, with a little satisfaction. Paul looked disappointed.

"It was impossible to miss the giant steel cage toward the rear of the boat, and I looked around for a place to run. Of course, Drew's VIP status meant that we were whirled through trainings and equipment fittings and signing waivers. We were headed back out onto the water before I even knew what hit me. Crazy Carl gave us his spiel, explaining how we would get into the cage, how it would be lowered, and what we could expect to see. I was about to pee my pants. Once we got to our spot, Drew just jumped right into the cage as it was lowered into the water, and I stood on the edge of the boat. *This defies human nature*, I thought. *People aren't meant to intentionally dive into water to be eaten by sharks*, I thought. Drew's head was popping out of the water, and Crazy Carl was getting impatient. So I jumped."

"You jumped into a cage surrounded by sharks?" Paul exclaimed, clearly impressed. Scotty nodded.

"I felt so heavy with all of my equipment on. I felt weighed down and awkward. And I was terrified. Beyond terrified. But I . . . "

"Jumped anyway," Brittany finished.

"I jumped anyway," Scotty smiled. "And out of everything I learned with Drew, that moment was probably the most defining. I was out of my element, uncomfortable, scared, weighed down, and unsure of what to expect. But I jumped anyway. I sank down into the cage. Thankfully this excursion didn't require us to stay submerged. We were bobbing on the surface of the water, our bodies protected by the cage. We could put our heads underwater and look around. But still. Terrifying.

"It was silent, but so beautifully blue. I had no idea that all of that beauty was literally one step out of my comfort zone. All of that beauty was just on the other side of my fear. The blueness went on for as far as I could see. I couldn't see the bottom, and other than a few small fish and seaweed floating around, it was like a blank canvas. I looked around and saw plenty of fish but I didn't see any sharks, and was temporarily relieved, but a little disappointed. I came back up for air and Drew gave me a thumbs-up.

"Drew stuck the snorkel in his mouth and put his face in the water. I did the same. We waited in stillness, until Drew started to point at something. All of a sudden three huge sharks came gliding toward us. I could hear the theme music from *Jaws* ringing in my ears. I also remember thinking, *Can't sharks sense fear?* If I could hear my heart beating in my ears, then they could, too. I instinctively grabbed Drew's arm and shot my head out of the water. But then I realized that not seeing was worse than seeing, so I put my head back in. I let go of Drew's arm and held on to the cage. I could not believe these giant creatures were a mere foot from me."

"Did you crap your swim trunks?" Paul interrupted, looking like a deer in headlights.

"Not quite, but I was more scared than I had ever been in my entire life. But as time went by, I became a little more confident. Crazy Carl must have thrown some fish into the water because the sharks raced toward the floating debris, their razor-sharp teeth just inches from my face. After circling a bit, they ripped into that fish like nobody's business. They attacked with a purpose. And it was like there was a hierarchy between them that only they understood. They didn't take the bait timidly. They went for what they wanted with power and purpose. They were confident in their ability and didn't second-guess themselves once they had investigated. They swam by us a few times but never really seemed aggressive toward us in the cage. It's like they knew the deal; you could tell they were smart but also gentle in a way. After a while, I almost felt like I could pet one once it was done eating. It seemed really calm before and after it fed.

> "They went for what they want with power and purpose. They were confident in their ability and didn't second-guess themselves once they had investigated."

"It's like they were 'hangry.' I can get hangry, too," Scotty joked. "I noticed that the sharks were oblivious to what was beneath them. They focused on what was in front of and above them. That was the coolest part. Sharks only look up; they never look down. Always stay positive! It's one thing to see them in the aquarium, but to see them up close and in the wild was something else."

> "The sharks were oblivious to what was beneath them. They focused on what was in front of and above them."

"I still can't believe you swam with sharks," Paul exclaimed. "We gotta do that, Zach. Ask the Google thing where we can go cage diving. I gotta try this," he said, throwing his phone at Zach.

"So they're always moving, they never go backward, they always look up and never look down, they are curious, they are respectful, they are flexible… I get it! What else did good ol' Drew teach you about sharks?" Paul asked.

Scotty raised his eyebrows in surprise. *He's really listening to all of this!* Scotty thought to himself.

"Why are sharks impact players?" Scotty asked out loud, thinking back on the way Drew broke down the Sacred Six and how they each played a vital role in how we should operate. Scotty suddenly had an idea. He began to rummage through the cabinets and hidden spaces throughout the boat.

"What are you looking for?" Paul asked. Scotty didn't answer. He was on a mission to reinforce the message, just like Drew had been. As he opened up drawers and looked in beach bags, he found what he was looking for. He came back to the front of the boat and showed Paul what he had found.

"A bandana?" Paul asked, confused.

Scotty smiled and suddenly understood why Drew found so much pleasure in teaching these lessons. Scotty stepped behind Paul and put the bandana around Paul's eyes.

"Woah woah, Scotty boy. You're not gonna feed me to the sharks, are you?" Paul laughed nervously.

Scotty quietly backed away from Paul and motioned for Zach to follow him toward the back of the boat, where Brittany was sitting. They both moved quietly and sat down next to Brittany. Paul wrung his hands in nervousness.

"Where am I?" Scotty asked. Paul whirled around toward Scotty's voice.

"What is this?" Paul asked, starting to fumble with his bandana.

"Hey, hey, hey! Leave it on. Now, where is Zach?" Scotty asked as he gently pushed Zach to move into the captain's chair.

"Hello?" Zach asked, quietly. Paul shifted his body toward Zach's voice.

"You can't see us, right? But you know where we are. How?" Scotty asked.

"I can hear you, you son of a …"

"Right. Your sense of hearing is on overdrive because your sense of sight is compromised. What else do you hear?" Scotty asked. It was quiet for a while. Paul began to list off the things he could hear, some of which Scotty had to pay extra-close attention to to hear. The waves lapping up on the side of the boat, the way the keys jingled in the boat ignition. Birds. A siren back onshore.

"Can I take this off now?" Paul asked, pulling the bandana off his eyes and squinting in the sun. Scotty smiled.

"Sharks know where to hunt because they have been specifically designed with senses that help them not only survive, but thrive. A shark has a keen sense of hearing, and their sense of smell is impeccable. Put a drop of blood in twenty-five gallons of water and the shark will be able to pinpoint it. They have been given everything they need to be successful, they just need to use what they have," Scotty explained, taking the bandana from Paul.

"Drew taught it to me this way. He took me about as far away from the sharks as possible to learn one of the most important lessons about them. Didn't make sense then, but makes sense now. When I was at my lowest moment, I focused on what I didn't have in life; I didn't understand that I was already fully equipped to be very successful in life. I was always looking down. Sometimes you have to step away from a problem or situation to see it for what it really is. Drew let me sit on our previous lessons for a while, but a few days later he was back in the driveway. But this time, he wasn't alone. There, in the front seat, in all of her freckled glory, was CiCi. I was immediately aware of my scruffy face and couldn't remember if I had even brushed my teeth, and wished I had sprayed on some cologne. I opened the back door of the truck and scooted in. Man, was I happy to see Cici; seeing her was such a pleasant surprise. It's like I had finally focused on something other than my pain and poor circumstances. What you dwell on, you dwell in, you know what I mean?" Scotty asked, trying to read Paul's face.

"So as I get buckled in, Drew says, 'You're not going to say hello?' And my face got red.

"'Hey, CiCi,' I remember saying timidly, admiring the way her curls fell down her back. Which led my eyes to her tank top and her shoulders and … " Scotty trailed off.

"Okay, Dad. We get it," Brittany said, smiling.

"So we drove, and nobody said anything. Her hair smelled good, like she had just taken a shower. Anyway, we were headed away from the coast. The road became narrower and I noticed that we were headed into the woods. The canopy of the trees blocked most of the sunlight, making it noticeably darker and cooler than the coast. We drove down narrow, winding roads that gradually took us deeper and deeper into the woods.

"We drove for what felt like an hour, but who knows how long it was? I just stared at the back of Cici's head. My stomach eventually started rumbling and I was anxious to get where we were going. I realized that I wasn't scared or nervous. By this time, I almost totally trusted Drew; I knew he knew what he was doing and was trying to teach me something. Then, out of nowhere, Drew slammed on the breaks. I looked around to see if he was trying to keep from hitting an animal, but we were alone. Drew put the truck in park, got out, and came around to my side. He opened the back door and pulled me out. He shoved a tan canvas bag into my chest and said, 'It'll be getting dark soon. The bears'll be hungry. You have everything you need to be successful. You just have to use what you have,' and winked. I started to ask questions, but Drew ran around the side of the truck, jumped in, and peeled out."

"He left you in the middle of the woods?" Zach exclaimed, scooting closer.

"Sure did. I chased after the truck but he was off. I watched the taillights fade in the distance and noticed that a tiny arm was stuck out the passenger side window. Waving." Scotty laughed. "I stood there, confused. I remember thinking, *This is what I get for trusting someone. They all turn out crazy. And now crazy and his beautiful daughter have left me out here to be bear food.* I hoped that Cici wasn't as crazy as her dear ol' dad, and that hopefully this wasn't her idea of flirting.

"So, I instantly quieted my mind and I dumped the bag out at my feet. There was a flashlight, a compass, a bottle of water, a brass skeleton key, and a shark tooth. I looked at each item carefully. I packed everything up and ran down the path where the car had gone. I didn't know where I was going, but I knew how to take the first step. So I did."

"I can't believe he just up and left you out there in the woods like that," Paul said, surprised. Scotty smiled, thinking back to how every element of Drew's lessons was intentional and deliberate. Everything he did had a purpose and a plan. But this was a big one, because he had never left Scotty alone as a part of his teachings.

Scotty recounted how he walked for what felt like hours. He actually went back and measured the distance a few years later, and it was 2.3 miles from where Drew dropped him off to where he had to make his first decision. Scotty stopped at an intersection. Two wooden signs pointed in opposite directions; one had the word *fear* etched into it and the other read *familiar*. He took out the compass, looking for clues on which way to go. It wasn't much help, so he put it back. It was getting dark, so he pulled out the flashlight and switched it on. He noticed something written on the handle of the flashlight. It was faded and hard to read, but Scotty figured out that it said, "Facing the fear is faster."

"'Facing the fear is faster'? What's that supposed to mean?" Paul asked. Scotty shrugged playfully.

"So I shined the light on the sign that said fear, and then on familiar, and then back to fear. *Facing the fear is faster?* I remember thinking. *Faster than what?* I knew I didn't have much more time to wait, so I made a decision and headed in the direction that *fear* was pointing toward. I quickly noticed a chill in the air and that I was depending more and more on my flashlight to see the steps ahead of me. I picked up my pace after I heard the bushes next to me rattle in the darkness. I began to take a mental inventory of what I had in my bag, mainly just to keep my mind busy. Then, I heard something. *Frogs?* Lots of frogs croaking—it was almost deafening. *Frogs mean water*, I thought as I ran toward the sound, unsure of what I was about to see. As I rounded a corner, the sound of the frog symphony became louder and a river came into focus. I stopped at the bank and shined my light across. I could see the other side, but it was at least 50 yards away. I shined my light to the left, then to the right, then back to the left. As the light swiped the river, something caught my eye. On the bank of the river, about 20 feet from me, was a structure. A small wooden shack, like an outhouse. I walked toward it, my heart racing. I noticed a wooden door and tried to open it, but of course …"

"Use the key!" Zach said, sitting on the edge of his seat.

"It was locked. So I dropped my bag and tried to rummage through it while holding the flashlight in my teeth, careful not to let it fall into the water. I dug through the bag and found the key. I grabbed it and pulled it out of the bag. I didn't notice my hands were shaking until I was trying to put the key into the lock. The key clicked, the door unlocked, and I opened the door and shined my light inside. A canoe. A single, rickety, questionable, old canoe with one oar. I stepped into the shack and pulled out the heavy boat and let it thud onto the bank. I closed the door to the shack, put the key back in the bag, and pushed the boat into the water. I jumped in, doing my best to keep my shoes and socks from getting wet. I used the oar to direct the boat through the calm water, suddenly aware of a slight current. I put the oar deep into the water until it hit the ground, and used the leverage of the sandy river bottom to help me navigate toward the opposite side. By the time I got to the other side, my arms were sore and the flashing light of my flashlight let me know that the batteries were dying.

"I pulled the boat up onto the shore and climbed on all fours up the riverbank. When I reached the top, I was in a large clearing, like a field. I was suddenly thankful for the water and chugged the entire bottle. I looked through the clearing and squinted my eyes at what looked like a pencil-thin line of smoke rising in the distance. I pulled the compass out again. I wasn't sure which way I was supposed to go, but I noticed something sketched into the back of the compass. It was a picture of a small farmhouse, with a chimney. And smoke rising from the chimney. There wasn't much detail and it was hard to see, but under the farmhouse it looked like someone had etched in a series of letters. It was too dark to see at this point, and my flashlight was fading. I rubbed my fingers over the letters and closed my eyes. I traced each letter, allowing the feeling from my fingers to send a message to my brain. I traced and retraced until something clicked. It was the letter G. Then an O. Then a W. I kept tracing and was pretty sure I felt an S. And then a T."

"G-o-w-s-t?" Paul asked, confused.

"Right. It didn't make sense to me either. But I kept tracing then I felt something I had missed. An E. G-O-W-E-S-T. Go west! I literally jumped up and down when I figured it out. I turned the compass around until I was facing west. When the compass needle settled, I was facing the smoke. So I ran as fast as I could through the clearing toward the smoke. As I got closer I could smell firewood burning, and then the farmhouse, with the smoking chimney, came into focus. I hooted and hollered and ran through the darkness toward the dimly lit front porch. There, on the porch, was Drew rocking in a rocking chair, with CiCi rocking next to him. I wasn't even worried about looking cool in front of her at this point and could have cared less about how I smelled or if I had in fact brushed my teeth. I launched myself toward the front porch and collapsed on the steps. Drew reached down to help me up and handed me a steaming cup of hot chocolate.

"I was feeling a little iffy and at this point I didn't know for sure if Drew and Cici were deranged or crazy or weird. For a moment the feelings of insecurity and abandonment from the days my parents would leave me alone crept up, but I thought about where I was and who I was with and pressed the feelings down. Drew was quiet for a second, sensing my anxiety, and then said, 'Sharks are impact players in the ocean because they have everything they need to be successful. They rely on their instincts and their senses to be successful. You had everything you needed, and you made the choice to use them.'

"'Choice?!' I remember yelling, spilling some hot chocolate on my pants. 'I didn't have a choice! You left me out there to die! What was I supposed to do? Lay down and let the bears get me?' I said, shouting this time. Drew wasn't fazed by my outburst. It was almost a flashback of the many times I got into it with my dad. I thought Drew was different, but it felt so familiar. I had thought this guy was different, but I had this sinking feeling that yet again, I had trusted someone who just wanted to play games. Almost ready to lose it, I suddenly realized CiCi was watching me, and I caught myself from my own rage. She smiled at me, and I became instantly embarrassed and sat down. She said, 'I am proud of you, Scotty. You did great!' and slowly I calmed down.

"I just sat down and took it all in; my fear had paralyzed me so much that I didn't realize that I had done something amazing. Her smile brought me joy and comfort all at the same time. I replied those five words over and over in my head: *I am proud of you.* I had never heard anyone say those words to me in my life. My emotions were all over the place, but I snapped back to reality as Drew started saying again that sharks are impact players because they have excellent senses, with a killer instinct that has helped them hold on to their spot as the ocean's top predator. I was thankful that Drew changed the vibe, because I was terrified that I might cry. With my dad, he was always a yeller, and he never showed compassion or love for anything or anybody. He thought the sight of a man crying was disgusting and weak. He always told me as a little boy to stop crying and toughen up. Just thinking of him made me mad, so I focused on CiCi's freckles.

"*I am proud of you.* I had never heard anyone say those words to me in my life."

"Drew sipped his hot chocolate. 'Scotty, you are growing, my man; soon you will learn the final sacred truth of the Sacred Six. So let us review. How did you know where to go?' Drew asked me, eager to hear my story. This was typical of Drew, always staying focused on the reinforcements, always making sure that those he was training and developing were understanding the lessons and information presented to them. So I thought back to where my adventure began and said, 'I went in the direction of your car.'

"'How'd you know to do that?' Drew asked, taking another sip.

"I shrugged. 'It just made sense. To get where you were I had to follow you.'

"'And then what?' Drew asked.

"'I walked until I got to the intersection. It said, *Fear is faster?* I said, more as a question than a statement.

"'Facing your fear is faster. If you had turned toward familiar, you wouldn't be here yet. There's a bridge and a lighted path that way, but it's much longer. The fear path is much faster but has some obstacles. In life, you get somewhere much faster if you feel the fear and take action anyway. Facing the fear is always a faster way to get where you're trying to go than sticking with what is familiar. Then what'd you do?' Drew asked.

> "Facing the fear is always a faster way to get where you're trying to go than sticking with what is familiar."

"That was a lot to take in, and it took me a second to process. 'Then I got to the river … '

"'How'd you get there?' Drew asked.

"'I heard the frogs.'

"'So your senses were heightened because you were in a serious situation. You've probably heard those frogs a million times and didn't even notice the sound. You trusted your senses. Then what?'

"'I got to the little shack and used the key to open its door. Got the boat, made it across. Found the message on the back of the compass. By touch. I couldn't see it, but I felt it,' I said, as it was all starting to make sense.

"'And I smelled the smoke. And I saw the tiny smoke line in the distance. More senses,' I realized. Drew rocked and smiled.

"'Sharks follow their intuition. They have everything they need. You had everything you needed. You did it,' Drew said, rocking slowly in the chair. 'Here is the lesson, son.'

"*Son? He called me son?* I thought. There was no holding back the tears at this point. I pretended to mess with my shoelaces to avoid eye contact and carefully wipe the tears away. 'Why is a shark called a shark and not another fish? What makes them different?' Drew asked. I was stumped.

"'Sharks are made of cartilage, remember? They don't have a bone in their body—which means, *sharks are flexible*. Sharks can adapt and change based on each situation. Some sharks can even operate in freshwater *and* saltwater. Always be flexible, son. When something isn't working, change. Fish hate change because their bones make them rigid. Sharks are impact players in the ocean because they are flexible. And that's number five. Sharks are flexible. I see the change in you daily. I'm proud of how far you have come in so little time. You are a special kid. I talk about you all the time.' I shot a glance over at CiCi, who smiled and nodded in agreement.

"Always be flexible, son. When something isn't working, change."

"Drew stood up and held the screen door open, motioning for CiCi and me to come inside. I took a long, hot shower and got myself back together. Drew made hot dogs and mac and cheese and we sat out on the porch and ate, as I told them more about my adventure. As I retold the story, I realized that as a shark, I could be in total control. I could change my future and my past wouldn't define me. Just as I thought that the day couldn't get any better, I became aware of CiCi's focus on me. She kept looking at me. I tried to stay focused on my story, but there was a moment where I looked at her and we locked eyes and I lost all train of thought. I was blubbering and stuttering, and I know I looked like a fool. I'll never forget her shy little smile and the way she wouldn't break eye contact. It was at that moment that I knew she was it for me. I stared right back. At that point, I didn't even care anymore. That was maybe the greatest day of my life. I was happy—I mean really happy. The inner peace I felt for the first time in my life felt so good and right.

> "I could change my future and my past wouldn't define me."

"Drew took our little moment as a sign that it was time to go, so we got cleaned up and packed up our stuff. As we were loading the truck, Drew asked a question: 'Scotty, as you look back on your day, why you would say you were successful in today's challenge?

> "As a shark in training, it is important to always be open to self-reflection and self-analysis so you can work on your strengths and weaknesses."

As a shark in training, it is important to always be open to self-reflection and self-analysis so you can work on your strengths and weaknesses.'

"I felt the blood rush to my face. I didn't mind these intellectual lessons when we were alone, but having CiCi there made me feel nervous and intimidated. I took a deep breath and said, 'Number one, I never stopped moving forward. Number two, I was always curious and thinking. Number three, I was flexible and in the moment. Number four, I stayed positive and focused on what I could do and what I knew instead of what I didn't.'

"'Very good. That is—" Drew started, but I interrupted him.

"'Number five. I trust and respect you, Drew, and I knew that this was all for my benefit. I saw it as an opportunity to be more like you, which pushed me to keep going,' I said, closing the liftgate on the truck. Out of the corner of my eye I could see him looking at me, but I kept my focus on my dirty tennis shoes and pushed stones around with my feet.

"It was quiet for a second, and when I finally looked up and locked eyes with Drew, he said, 'I am sure today wasn't easy for you, son. But I am so proud of you and excited for your future.' We smiled at each other, and I went around the truck and to the rear door.

"'Sit up here with us?' CiCi said as I opened the back door of the truck. She said it like a question, but the way she looked at me when she said it told me that it wasn't a question. I shot a look at Drew, who shrugged and put the key in the ignition. I shut the back door and CiCi scooted over toward her dad. I jumped in next to her, careful not to touch her. I sat like a statue, eyes facing front, both overjoyed and terrified at the same time. Drew turned on the radio, and tapped his fingers on the steering wheel as "Dancing on the Ceiling" played. We drove through the dark woods in silence, other than the sound of the radio. We stopped at a little gas station in the middle of nowhere and Drew went inside to pay. As soon as he was inside, I felt something brush up against my hand. I kept my eyes facing forward, unsure of what was happening. Then I felt it again, this time more intentional. I looked down and CiCi, also looking straight ahead, was inching her pinky finger toward mine. I moved my finger ever so slowly toward hers, and she linked her pinky finger with mine. I looked over at her and smiled, and she blushed. We rode like that the rest of the way. As we drove into darkness, I began to understand the magnitude of the day. I had not only found my way through the woods with very basic supplies, but I also knew five of the Sacred Six, and I was pretty confident that CiCi was officially my girl. I felt like a new man."

"Ooohh la la," joked Paul, making kissing sounds. Zach put some bait on the line and sent it reeling out into the water.

"When we got to my house, Drew put the truck in park, which he had never done before. He got out and came around and opened my door. He shut the door and we walked toward my front door in silence. He handed me the canvas bag and told me to keep it. Then he asked me what I was doing the next day. I shrugged, a little disappointed that he didn't have plans for me.

"'I have a position open at my shop, and it's yours if you want it. Pays well, flexible schedule. I'll teach you everything you need to know,' he said, putting his hand on my shoulder. I remember thinking he had already taught me so much. 'Think about it,' he said. 'I think you'd do great.' I went inside and went straight to bed, thinking about the way CiCi's hair smelled and kicking myself for not being the one who made the first pinky move. I replayed the entire day over and over, but always spent extra time thinking about the way she looked at me on the porch and the way she held my hand. *Is she my girl? What is the process for this? Are we a couple? Maybe it was an accident. Maybe I'm making it all up*, I fell asleep thinking, and smiling. I had never been this happy in my life. All my life I had wanted to know what real love was, what support was, what it meant to have a family and a father who taught you about life and mentored you and just loved you. I felt like I had gotten all of it in one day."

Scotty looked around the boat. Everyone was fully invested in this story, and the space in between Paul's interruptions let Scotty know that he was really listening and processing all of the information. He knew that he had taken control of the boat. But suddenly, Paul, as uncomfortable and confused as he could be, reached into the cooler and opened a beer. The crisp pop of the bottle cap stopped Scotty in his tracks. He was 13 years sober. Thirteen years, five months, and two days, to be exact, but the sound of the bottle opening brought him right back to his days before Drew, before Shark's, before CiCi and Brittany. The moment was intense, even though nobody said a word. A few moments passed, and Scotty was able to shake his feelings off and continue with his story. He knew that this was his boat now. He was the captain and in his mind he could hear his wife Cici cheering.

"So I was up bright and early the next day and rode my bike to Shark's. The look on Drew's face when I pulled up was one of relief and pride. He welcomed me into the shop, threw a white polo with a shark emblem on the breast pocket at me, and walked me into his office. The same office I'm in now, actually.

"'Are you a shark?' he asked me.

"'Yes!' I said enthusiastically.

"'Wrong,' he said, as if he had known that I was going to say yes.

"'Wrong? What are you talking about? I did all the things, I went in a freakin' shark cage. You left me in the woods!' I shrieked.

"'I told you from day one I see one when I look at you. But you're not there yet. You have to keep working until you master the mindset of a shark and operate like one naturally, every day. You have to put the things you've learned into practice. It doesn't happen overnight. Now you know what you need to do, and I'm here to help you get there. But you have to trust me and listen to me and follow my lead. When you are a shark, you don't just swim, you SWIM," he said.

"You have to keep working until you master the mindset of a shark and operate like one naturally, every day."

"He flipped to a blank sheet of paper in his notepad and pulled a pen from his shirt pocket. Drew kept teaching lessons because he understood how hard it was to really change. He had a habit of repeating himself and reinforcing his teachings. 'Once you master the Sacred Six and live them, that's when you SWIM, son,' he said, writing the phrase on the paper:

"Once you master the Sacred Six and live them, that's when you SWIM, son."

"*When you are a shark, you don't just swim, you SWIM!*

"He wrote the last word in all capital letters, underlined and circled it, making it very clear again that the way sharks swim is very different than the way fish swim. 'Oh, okay, I think I get it,' I said, looking from the paper up to Drew. 'Sharks are impact players in the ocean because they execute the Sacred Six naturally,' Drew explained. 'Once they become natural for you, you will SWIM, too.' This wouldn't be the last time Drew used the term *SWIM* to mean something far deeper than just cruising through the water. There would be many times during the three years that I worked for him that'd he remind me of what it meant to be a shark. The Sacred Six was more than just words to us at Shark's AC Repair Service; it was a way of life that we took very seriously—all of us, but nobody more than Drew. He was the head shark and to watch him operate was awesome," Scotty said, thinking back on the memory with fondness.

> "Sharks are impact players in the ocean because they execute the Sacred Six naturally."

"Sacred Six, SWIM, well ain't that a couple of cute little slogans. Guess it makes more sense when you see it on paper, huh?" Paul asked. Scotty was a little disappointed that the catchphrase didn't impact Paul the same way it had impacted him, but then again he wasn't surprised.

"So let me see if I got them all," Paul said, taking a deep breath. He tapped each one of his fingers as he listed each lesson.

"Sharks never stop moving forward," Paul said confidently.

"If they do, they die," Scotty added. "They focus on their future and not their past."

"Sharks always look up and never look down," Paul continued.

"Sharks are positive; they focus on what's above them and not what's beneath them."

"Sharks always recognize other sharks and respect their environment."

"They have been given everything they need to be successful, they just need to use what they have."

Scotty nodded in approval.

"Sharks can identify other sharks and respect them enough without perceiving their success or their mere existence as a threat," Paul said, feeling more accomplished than he had in a while.

"Finally," Paul took a deep breath, "**Sharks are curious; they are always learning."** Scotty noticed the look of pride on Paul's face. They are decisive but are aggressive once they are focused on their prey. **Sharks are flexible because they are made of cartilage.**" Scotty wanted to hug him, but held back. He couldn't believe that Paul actually remembered the five lessons he had heard so far. "So Scotty, I am curious. What is number six?" Paul asked. "And have you ever had shark fin soup? Not bad," he winked.

The two took in the moment silently. By the look on Paul's face, Scotty could tell he was thinking carefully about each lesson and story. Scotty was confident he had connected with Paul in a way like never before.

"Holy cow! I got something! What is that thing?" Zach yelled from the bow of the boat. Everyone rushed over to Zach's side. Zach was struggling with the fish on the line, so Paul snatched the reel and pulled in the thrashing creature.

"What *is* that?" Paul asked, pointing to the mysterious creature on the other end of the line.

"That, my friends, is a remora. Also known as a suckerfish," Scotty said with a smile.

"A sucker what?" Paul asked.

"No. Way," Brittany said, rushing back to Scotty's side because she knew what was next.

"A shark *and* a suckerfish?" she asked, looking directly into Scotty's eyes with amazement.

"Yeah," he replied, still astonished.

"What's the big deal?" Zach asked. "Let me guess, you've got a story about the suckerfish, too?"

Brittany knew that God had to be involved. You couldn't write this script any better.

"Well, guys, before I tell you about number six, you need to know about the suckerfish," Scotty began.

3

Going for a Ride

The remora fish was about two feet long. By the way Paul pulled it in with such ease, Scotty guessed it weighed less than three pounds.

"It's called a suckerfish," Scotty explained. "Its species-specific name is a remora. See that thing on the top of its head? It's like a suction cup. It attaches to other, bigger fish in the ocean, like sharks. The suckerfish and the shark have a mutually beneficial relationship. The suckerfish attaches to the shark and the shark takes it wherever it goes; suckerfish get free rides in the ocean and can conserve energy. Some remora fish can stay attached for as long as three months. **The shark takes care of the suckerfish.** Suckerfish benefit from the shark's protection and free rides in the ocean, and they get to eat the scraps of each kill," Scotty said, pointing out each part of the fish as he explained.

> "The suckerfish and the shark have a mutually beneficial relationship."

"But why do sharks allow this? What are the benefits to them?" Zach asked.

Scotty pointed at Zach and smiled approvingly, excited to dive deeper into the lesson. "Because parasites are also always trying to connect to a host. So the suckerfish eats the parasites that can be found on the shark's skin. If a parasite gets into a shark's gills it can affect its breathing or kill it. If the parasite gets into the shark's nostril it can attack its brain. No matter how powerful a shark is, a shark knows it needs help and good teammates to thrive.

> "No matter how powerful a shark is, a shark knows it needs help and good teammates to thrive."

"I always think of it like this: Beware of who you allow to connect to you. Sharks will take as many suckerfish as they can with them. It's a win-win-win. People are no different—who we connect with in life can make or break us," Scotty explained, casually taking the ugly fish off the line and holding it up for everyone to see. He took a second to take in the moment, still amazed at how he had learned so much about life from an ugly fish and a man who saw something in him that he didn't see himself.

> "Beware of who you allow to connect to you … who we connect with in life can make or break us."

He continued:

"Another cool thing—some remoras even attach and live inside the shark's mouth. Talk about trust! The shark could chomp down and devour the vulnerable fish, but it doesn't. The relationship is built on trust, experience, and understanding the mutual connection."

For a while, everyone on the boat was quiet.

"I started working at Drew's that Monday after the adventure in the woods. Each day I'd show up and he'd show me around, walk me through certain aspects of the shop, explain equipment to me. There were about twenty other guys who worked there, and he introduced me to all of them. They all had a story. Some were recovering drug addicts, others had done jail time. Some had been homeless. Everyone came with baggage and scars. It made me feel less self-conscious about my past, since each of them had one too. I'd eventually learn that our messes and our hurts and mistakes helped create a solid bond between us. We felt taken care of for the first time in our lives—at least I did. But that is the kind of guy Drew was, always looking out for others. And what I didn't know then, but would eventually learn, was that Drew needed us as much as we needed him.

"It was like the time he picked me up on a Sunday morning and suggested we go for a drive. I noticed that we had passed the exit for the shop, and I had a feeling I was in for another lesson. We drove to the next town over and pulled down a gravel road. We passed a sign that said *Animal Rescue* in big black letters, with *Adoptions Today* written in marker under it. We parked and I could hear dogs barking from inside. We walked in and it smelled like dog food and hand sanitizer. Glass cages lined the walls, some empty and some home to sleeping puppies. A few dogs paced their tiny cubicle, barking and pawing at the glass. Toward the back of the building, bigger, sadder-looking dogs laid quietly in their metal cages, thumping their tails as we got closer.

"'Can I help you?' a peppy volunteer asked, standing next to us and admiring the poodle in the cage in front of us.

"'Yes, actually. We're here for the worst dog you've got. The one who's been here the longest. The ugliest one, the most hopeless one. He's ours,' Drew said, like he was picking out a brand-new car that had to be perfect. He wanted the dog that nobody else wanted.

"'Really?' the girl squealed, throwing her hands in the air. 'You're here for Sherbert! I'll go get him!' she said and hopped down the hall. Drew looked at me and raised his eyebrows. *Who names a dog Sherbert?*

"She called for us from the back of the building, and we followed. She put her back against the door to prop it open, kneeled down, and calmly and quietly coaxed Sherbert from the back. After some persuasion and the promise of treats, Sherbert appeared. He looked like he had never had a bath. His fur was patchy, his eyes were sad, and his tail was between his three legs. Yes, this raggedy dog had only three legs. Drew looked like he had won the lottery. He got down on the floor and called Sherbert over, and the dog took slow, careful, timid steps toward Drew's outstretched hand. It took about 10 minutes, but finally Sherbert laid down next to Drew and let him gently stroke his matted fur.

"'His day was tomorrow.' The girl pouted, and then smiled. 'You're saving him,' she said sweetly. I looked around at all of the animals and felt a mix of emotions. I was hopeful for their future but sad for their past. They each had a story; many of them had been abandoned, forgotten about, discarded. I knew the feeling. I wanted to save them all. Like he had read my mind, Drew said, 'We can't save them all, but we can save one. We can't change the world for all of them, but we can change the world for one of them, and that's powerful.'

> "We can't change the world for all of them, but we can change the world for one of them, and that's powerful."

We spent the next half hour on the floor next to this dog. Drew spoke to him softly, promising him a warm place to sleep, a shop full of guys who would love him unconditionally. We bought dog treats and a soft new dog bed and clipped a leash to Sherbert's collar. He walked outside with us, limping slightly and overwhelmed by the sounds and smells of the outdoors. Eventually we got him in the truck, and he laid right down. The associate waved to us from the parking lot and we headed home.

"'Well, we sure as hell aren't calling you Sherbert. Who names their dog Sherbert?' Drew laughed, putting one hand on the dog's head. We drove in silence for a while, both of us resting our hands on the dog's back.

"'Angel, Bull, Goblin, Nurse, Great White, Hammerhead…' Drew said out loud, clearly naming different types of sharks, 'Tiger, Mako, Whale…'

"'His tail!' I said, pointing at the splotchy tail that was slowly thumping against the seat.

"'When you said Mako, he wagged his tail!' I said excitedly.

"'Mako? You like that, boy?' Drew asked. The dog lifted his head.

"'Mako it is!' Drew said, playfully ruffling the fur on top of the dog's head.

"On Monday, the guys were all thrilled to meet Mako. They all sat on the floor of shop, holding their hands out for Mako to smell. He was still shy and unsure, but it was like he connected with the guys. As I stood back and watched, I suddenly realized why Drew chose Mako. It was because he was broken, and he knew all of us could relate to him. We all connected over our messy pasts, our scars, our injuries, and our damages. Mako fit in perfectly with us because he didn't fit in anywhere else, and we could relate.

"Getting Mako was a lesson that required very little explaining. Drew didn't have to tell me why he was doing what he was doing; I just knew. It was the kind of person, the kind of shark that Drew was. He believed in the underdog and he believed in second chances and finding hope in a hopeless situation. He had rescued all of us just like he had rescued Mako, and it made everyone better in the long run.

"Mako was a shop dog for the rest of his life; he was a part of the family and a constant reminder that we can choose to see beauty in the mess." Scotty smiled, and suddenly felt pulled to get another dog for the shop. "Mako followed Drew around like his little shadow, and when Mako would roll over for a belly rub, Drew would always say, 'Who saved who, huh, buddy?' It would always remind me that we needed Mako just as much as he needed us. Without ever having to say it, Drew taught me that sharks know they need suckerfish. The suckerfish keeps the shark humble and balances the playing field. Drew took Mako in—all of us, for that matter—because it made his heart feel good.

"His heart for all of us, his determination to rescue the broken and the jacked up, was a true reflection of his strength. That's the magic of Drew; he needed the techs as much as they needed him. He needed the three-legged dog just as much as the three-legged dog needed him. The beauty of the shark and suckerfish relationship is that both parties add value, which reminds me of another Drewism. He'd always say, 'We're not in the AC business, we're in the people business.' He enjoyed serving people; the money we made was always secondary.

> "He'd always say, 'We're not in the AC business, we're in the people business.' He enjoyed serving people; the money we made was always secondary."

"On Friday of the first week, Drew met me at the front door of the shop first thing in the morning. He told me to hop in the truck, gave a few orders to the guys in the shop, and told them he'd be back in time for closing. We drove through town, then across the tracks, so to speak, toward the more affluent part of town. Quiet, tree-lined roads, gated communities, BMWs and Mercedes cruising through the streets. Men in expensive suits with briefcases walking into office buildings, moms dressed to the nines pushing kids in strollers through the park. We turned into a gated community and the guard at the front waved us in. We drove down windy roads, and as we went deeper into the neighborhood, the houses got bigger. We pulled into a driveway and I was speechless. Compared to my little shack of a house, this was a freakin' mansion. Drew got out, and I followed him to the door, curious as to which one of our customers lived here. To my surprise, he pulled out a key and walked right in the front door.

"'Is this your house?' I asked, looking up at the grand architecture. Drew nodded and welcomed me in.

"'Head back out to the pool. I'm going to change and I'll meet you out there,' he said, disappearing up the spiral staircase. I walked carefully through the grand foyer, into a living room bigger than my entire house, and out the sliding glass doors to the pool. There was a waterfall feature, sport court, and outdoor kitchen. *Why do they have their kitchen outside?* I remember thinking. Drew came out soon after, and I followed him around the pool, across the patio, and past the tiki hut. I followed him to the gorgeous pale blue fishing boat parked at the dock right behind the house, and when he got in, I did, too. A lot of what Drew did was in silence. I just watched and followed. I had learned to wait to ask questions because, more often than not, Drew was already planning on answering them. We slowly moved through the channel out to open water, where Drew baited the line and cast it overboard.

"'The remora fish aren't really picky; they'll eat pretty much anything. But they don't travel in schools, so they can be kinda hard to find and catch. They are loners and they live out in the deeper parts of ocean, away from the shore. But we'll try,' he said, taking a seat.

"'A remora?' I asked, curiously.

"'You'll see,' Drew said as he put his feet up, laced his hands behind his head, and closed his eyes. I kept an eye on the line and waited. A tug on the line caused Drew to jump to his feet and grab the rod. He reeled in the line with ease and brought up a sparkling mackerel.

"'Eh,' Drew said, and tossed the fish back into the water. 'The only way you can eat those is to smoke them.' I watched the fish swim away while Drew put fresh bait on the line, cast it overboard, and reclaimed his spot in the captain's chair. Again, he put his feet back up and closed his eyes.

"A while later, the line tugged again. We both rushed to the side, and Drew reeled and pulled the line, anxious to see what was on the other side. This time, the challenger on the other end of the line was bigger, stronger. It took Drew a good while to bring it on board.

"'A grunt,' he said, disappointed. The large fish flapped and thrashed out of water. Drew unhooked it, and, to my surprise, threw it back.

"'What are you doing?' I asked him, shocked.

"'Not what I'm looking for. Good, but not good for what I'm trying to do. It can't help me with this lesson. We'll wait,' he said, retreating back to his seat.

"Finally, after about three hours, the tug on the line brought more success. Drew pulled up the line and shouted as he pulled the ugliest fish I had ever seen on board. *We threw away some beautiful fish for this?* I remember thinking.

"Drew reminded me about how the remora, the suckerfish, attaches itself to host, typically a shark. The shark provides transportation for the suckerfish and a constant flow of water over its gills that keep it alive," Scotty explained.

"If I was a shark, I wouldn't let this ugly, small thing mooch off me. I'd tell that ocean leech to get off me, to find its own way," Zach said with a bit of disgust in his voice. "Sharks are sharks because they're alpha, like you said. Little fish like this don't get a free ride," he said with confidence, looking over at Paul for approval. Paul smiled and nodded at his son in pride.

"Remember," Scotty interjected, "the suckerfish isn't getting a free ride, and the shark benefits in a lot of ways by keeping it around. Suckerfish add value to the shark, but, most importantly, the suckerfish keep the shark alive. The shark provides protection, and the suckerfish eats the bacteria and parasites off the shark. Sharks are alpha, but they also recognize a mutually beneficial relationship when they see one, and they take advantage of it," Scotty said matter-of-factly.

Scotty went back to his story. "As Drew and I examined that suckerfish, Drew explained that the shark's position in the ocean's hierarchy is not diminished simply because it's got a tagalong. Allowing the suckerfish to go for a ride is actually a *smart* decision on the shark's part. It's like a powerful business relationship because it keeps the shark in its best possible state," Scotty explained, dipping a large five-gallon bucket over the side of the boat and gently putting the suckerfish into it.

"Allowing the suckerfish to go for a ride is actually a *smart* decision on the shark's part. It's like a powerful business relationship because it keeps the shark in its best possible state."

"It's not a sign of weakness to associate with someone who is smaller or less experienced or less capable than you are," Brittany added, glaring over at Zach.

"Right. But it's kind of lazy, you know? Just latching onto someone who has worked their entire life to reach the top?" Zach countered, almost daring Brittany to come back at him.

Paul thought for a second. His son had a point. Paul had worked tirelessly to get to where he was, and he didn't rely on money or help from anyone else to do it. Sure, he had burned bridges and had had to play a little dirty to get to where he was, but it was all in the name of business. Nothing personal. Scotty was the one who had accepted a handout from Drew and that was fine, but it didn't quite make him a shark. *I'm the one who went off and did big things. Me. On my own,* Paul thought to himself. *That's what a shark does, figures it out on its own. I didn't need anyone's help; I am a self-made man.*

"Not lazy," Scotty replied, "Smart. A suckerfish knows it can thrive by attaching itself to a shark. It knows it is protected, it is fed, it's safe. And it benefits the shark, too. That's the part you're missing. It's not lazy, it's an intentional move to survive and thrive that benefits *both* parties," Scotty said, slowly. "We all have strengths and weaknesses. A shark, a *real* shark, even understands its own limitations."

"We all have strengths and weaknesses. A shark, a *real* shark, even understands its own limitations."

"So take this to the real world," Zach said, still not convinced. "Let's say Drew's the shark and now you're his suckerfish," Zach said boldly, almost condescendingly. "Following him around, in his shadow. How do *you* benefit *him*?" Zach asked, staring at Scotty.

"Great question. At first, I was unsure, too. How was I, this punk kid with family issues and a mug shot, going to do anything even close to benefiting Drew? It was humbling and intimidating. Made me feel insecure at first.

"I learned all about the shark in a matter of days. And I learned a lot about the suckerfish on that boat trip. But it would take me years to develop a true understanding of this unique, natural relationship and how it would help launch me into the man I am today," Scotty said, smiling. "As I really learned how to run a business, I learned that companies with mentoring programs are more productive and have lower turnover. I encourage all of my techs to find someone they admire, someone more successful than they are, to help them learn and grow. Having Drew as a mentor literally changed my life and the trajectory of the business. I can't stress enough the power that mentorship has in a thriving business. You can reduce attrition, improve job performance, and improve productivity, and mentors are more likely to get promoted, too. Paul, you had a mentor, right?" Scotty asked, pretty sure he already knew the answer.

> "I can't stress enough the power that mentorship has in a thriving business. You can reduce attrition, improve job performance, and improve productivity, and mentors are more likely to get promoted, too."

Paul blankly looked at Scotty. He thought about the older businesspeople who had influenced him early in his career, the leaders who had let him learn from their mistakes. It was those same people who later warned him, with honesty and love, about how his attitude and some questionable business practices could come back to hurt him. When they would offer honest, constructive criticism that hurt a little bit, he would always say they were just old and outdated and stopped listening to them altogether. *I don't know much about this whole mentorship thing,* he thought, *but I'm pretty sure that wasn't the way it was supposed to go.* Paul had never really been anyone's suckerfish.

When Paul didn't say anything about having a mentor, Scotty continued. "Working with Drew was one of the most educational experiences of my life. And I'm not talking about learning about coolers and coils. I'm talking about learning about a work ethic, building personal relationships, doing work that mattered. I remember him telling me, 'Our chief want in life is somebody who will make us do what we can.' Later I learned it was really Ralph Waldo Emerson who said it first, but at the moment I was very impressed with Drew's eloquence and wisdom." Scotty laughed.

"And that is what Drew did. He showed me what I was capable of. And there is power in that. When you feel like someone is in your corner, when someone sees something in you that you don't, you're much more likely to work toward becoming that person, even if you don't see it. And Drew always reminded me that, just like the shark and the suckerfish's mutually beneficial relationship, he was getting as much from me being around as I was. Before I became the CEO, Drew grew us into a $5,000,000 company operating in Broward only. Oh, Drew benefited from his suckerfish big time. He grew his company into a family culture using misfits and transformed us into husbands, fathers, and entrepreneurs—"

"Wait, wait, wait," Zach interrupted. "You're a CEO of a $5,000,000 company?" Zach looked over at Paul, who looked like a deer in headlights.

Scotty hesitated. It wasn't his nature to discuss money and income, but it was too late now. He preferred his lifestyle to be what impacted people, not his bank account.

"Well, I . . . ," Scotty started.

"No, actually he's the CEO of a $25,000,000 company that covers not only Broward but Dade and Palm Beach counties, too," Brittany chimed in. The expression on Paul's face made the entire trip worth it, for Brittany at least.

"Bottom line is this," Scotty said, shifting the focus from his bank account to the actual lesson, "sharks and suckerfish need each other. Everyone understand?"

Everyone on the boat nodded in agreement. Since he had everyone's attention, he continued.

"I was there when Drew got his first cell phone. We stayed in the shop way after closing, me teaching him how to input all his contacts. He wanted to go through each ringtone and assign each one to a different person. I showed him how to adjust the volume, all of it. As we left the shop that day, he said, 'Thanks, suckerfish, for all your help tonight." It was the first time he actually referred to me as a suckerfish. I mean, I kind of figured that that was my role, but it was the first time I had a real, tangible example of how this relationship was mutually beneficial." Scotty smiled. He remembered getting home that night, smiling and then laughing at how crazy it was that someone had referred to him as an ugly fish and how good it had made him feel.

"I began to notice some outdated techniques that Drew was using to collect payments. We all realized that many people owed Drew money—he'd either forgot to collect a payment or avoided hounding people for money. Many people took advantage of Drew's heart. So we protected Drew from parasites. We taught him how to send out invoices electronically; they were automated until the client settled up. We even talked Drew into offering a service plan, where we would visit our clients once a quarter to check on things. That was a huge profit for the business, with passive income. We wondered how Drew was so successful, yet never used any technology. 'I'm old school!' Drew would respond when the guys would playfully make fun of him for writing everything down in his raggedy old planner. All the techs chipped in and bought Drew's first computer for his birthday. We loved Drew and he loved us.

"I knew my way around computers because we used them at the Boys and Girls Club every day after school, so I stayed late to help set up Drew's computer and show him the basics. I slowly showed him how we could use the latest software to totally run the entire business. Thankfully, Drew had a sense of humor and could make fun of himself, because his journey to understanding and using technology in the office was a slow one. Drew was open-minded to change and always willing to hear the ideas of the younger, 'hipper' employees. I'm sure that implementing new strategies and technology into the shop is what helped launch Sharks into the company it is today. Drew's willingness to listen to new ideas and my willingness to teach him resulted in major profit all around. Remember, sharks are flexible. And sharks need suckerfish and suckerfish need sharks. Today, Shark's AC Repair Service is basically a technology company. There is not a more advanced AC company or a company with a better culture in all of Florida, if not the country.

"I learned my biggest lesson after I had been on the job for a few months. It was the first time I really messed up, and my mistake cost the store a lot of money and a good customer. Basically I messed up on the draining system for a big unit; the tubing wasn't insulated properly and the customer suffered major water damage to their home. It was clearly a bonehead mistake, and I offered to pay for the repairs with payments from my paycheck. Drew was mad—pissed. I don't think it was about the money; it was the damage to the reputation of the company and losing a good customer with whom he had built a strong relationship. I was sure I was fired, and I avoided Drew all day. Then he called me in his office and pointed to the chair across from him. I sat.

"'Your mistake cost the company a lot of money, but more importantly it caused us to disappoint a client and cause them stress and unnecessary inconvenience,' Drew said to me, slowly and intensely.

"'I'll go,' I said, standing up, my fight-or-flight instinct kicking in. Drew pointed to the seat. I sat.

"'You don't get to run away from this. Our chief want in life is somebody who will make us do what we can. I am going to show you that you *can* fix this. That you *can* face this. I forgive you for this. I'm giving you grace, a second chance. An opportunity to make it right. You, suckerfish, are helping me to remember to really walk the talk, to execute the same fundamentals that I preach to all of you around here. We help each other, we need each other, we ..."

> "Our chief want in life is somebody who will make us do what we can."

"'Stand up for each other. Back each other up,' I finished for him. He nodded and gave me a small smile.

"'So we're going to fix this. All of us,' Drew said with determination. He stood up and walked out of the office, and I followed. He got in his truck and motioned for me to get in. I was surprised to see that the rest of the shop was empty, and even more surprised to see the rest of the guys in their trucks, revving and waiting for me. Drew led the way and we caravanned straight to the place of my botched AC job. My stomach was in my chest, but I watched all of the other guys get out of their trucks and wait for me. I felt protected, like I was surrounded by big brothers. Drew motioned at me to knock and I did, twice, and stepped back. The homeowner answered and, without a word or a smile, let us all in. We stood in the entryway of the home, and I could see contractors working on replacing the water-damaged floor behind him. We were silent, until someone not-too-subtly poked me in the back.

"'Mr. Davis, I'm really sorry for my mistake. I take full responsibility for the incorrect installation. My newness in the industry is no excuse for my mistake, and I'll do whatever it takes to make it right," I said, my voice trembling.

"Then Drew spoke. 'Clint, Scotty's a good kid and made an honest mistake. But his mistake is our mistake, and we are all here to formally apologize. We'd also like to cover the cost of the floor repair. And, if it is okay with you, we would like to send Scotty back out here, under my supervision, to fix his mistake,' Drew said with confidence.

"'Scotty's a good AC tech. One of the best we got,' said one of the guys from the back.

"'He's hard-working and always willing to learn. He comes early and stays late and we are proud of him and happy to have him on our team,' said someone else. Mr. Davis started to smile. Their kind words made me blush. I had thought they had my back, but that day I knew that they had my back for real—each and every one of them, including Tracey, vouched for me. I had never felt this way before. My bottom lip quivered as I shifted uncomfortably in my tennis shoes. This moment changed a lot for me. It is why I'm always looking for ways to encourage and speak light into people, because I remember how life-changing it was for me. I had screwed up, but fixing it felt good.

"'And,' Drew interjected, as he slid an envelope into my hand, 'Scotty wants to give you something,' he said as he nudged my elbow. I handed Mr. Davis the envelope and he opened it. It was a $100 gift card to a steakhouse down the street. He was impressed and thankful and open to letting me fix the mistake. As we caravanned back to the shop, I thanked Drew. He told me that we were family, and this rookie mistake helped him remember his first giant mistake and how he wished it had been handled. We cruised down the street back to the shop in formation, one huge shark in the front truck followed by a bunch of suckerfish cruising close by.

"'You, suckerfish, have helped me remember how far I've come, how blessed I am to have what I have and know what I know. You remind me of me when I was young, hungry, and determined. And I'm proud of what I've accomplished and what you're going to accomplish,' Drew said, as we drove back that day. I pretended not to notice his lip quivering a bit as he spoke, and for a second felt embarrassed for him. But when we stopped, he looked right at me with confidence, a single tear escaping his eye. He wasn't embarrassed at all. That's when I learned it was okay to be real and vulnerable and still be a man.

"'Here is number six of the Sacred Six, Scotty, are you ready?'

"'Yes sir!' I said excitedly.

"'Never forget this one, maybe the most important one. It is the one that most businesspeople miss: SHARKS. TAKE. CARE. OF. THEIR. SUCKERFISH AND ELEVATE THEM TO NEW LEVELS.' He paused between each word for emphasis. 'You are not a real success in my book until you take others with you. A great white shark can have like thirty suckerfish connected to him all at the same time, maybe more,' Drew said, turning his attention back to the road.

> "You are not a real success in my book until you take others with you."

"'And that $100? That will come from your next week's paycheck,' Drew said with a sly smile and a wink.

"'When you are a shark, you don't just swim, you SWIM. Any questions about the Sacred Six, Scotty?' Drew asked. I shook my head. 'No sir, I get it!' I said with confidence.

"'Repeat them again for me,' Drew asked. I recited the Sacred Six aloud and proudly I began to find myself saying almost every phrase Drew would say. I was definitely living inside this man's mouth and—"

"Hold up. What did you just say?" Zach asked, looking confused and shooting an amused look over at Paul. "Did you say you were living in his mouth? I don't know, man. I can do all of these little metaphors but living in someone's mouth?" he asked.

Scotty smiled. It was something he was so used to saying that he forgot that it sounded weird to other people.

"Living in someone's mouth. It's like the words that people say can give life. The things people say to and about us can impact us for a lifetime. When you live in someone's mouth, you take what they say as truth and then apply it to your life. And then you start saying it. Drew knew this, which is why he was so focused on making sure we not only knew the Sacred Six, but that we spoke them out loud every day.

> "The words that people say can give life. The things people say to and about us can impact us for a lifetime."

"The Sacred Six became a part of who we were because we heard them on a daily basis and knew them to be true. We have to be aware of those who are living in our mouths, too;

the people who are listening to what we say and even what we don't say, and are using our words to build their foundations. Make sense?" Scotty asked.

Zach looked at him with uncertainty. "I guess," he said slowly, "but it still sounds weird."

"Okay, okay, enough with being in someone's mouth," Paul said impatiently. "What happened when you got back to the shop?"

Scotty continued. "As we pulled in, I thanked each of the guys for sticking up for me, and they all made it seem like no big deal. As I was shaking hands with everyone and saying goodbye, a wave of brown curls caught my eye. CiCi's."

"At this point I had been working for Drew for about six months, and she'd make an occasional appearance at the shop. We'd talk and hang out, and then Drew would find something for me to do, and she'd go home. But she'd never shown up after work hours before. The other guys jumped in their cars and left, Drew walked into the shop to close up, and left CiCi and me outside.

"'Mr. Davis okay?' she asked me. I was humiliated that she knew about my mistake, and it must have shown on my face. Come to find out, Drew talked about me all the time at home.

"'Hey,' she said, putting her hand on my arm, 'everyone messes up, it's not a big deal. My dad loves you, he trusts you. Says you're like the son he never had." I breathed a sigh of relief.

"'Okay, we're all closed up. You ready, C?' Drew asked, heading toward the car. But CiCi didn't move. And to my surprise slash terror, her hand was still on my arm.

"'Actually, Dad, I think Scotty and I are going to walk up to Sawyer's for ice cream,' she said confidently.

"'Oh, is that right?' he asked, looking directly at me. I froze.

"'Yes... yes, sir. If that's okay with... you,' I stuttered. It was such an emotional day for me, a day I will never forget. I had learned how to be accountable, had learned number six, and now I was going on an actual date with a girl—and not just any girl, the girl of my dreams!" Scotty smiled inside.

"'I guess it's fine. Be home by seven,' Drew said, and jumped in his car. I took a deep breath and smiled at CiCi. We headed toward town, walking and laughing the entire way. I mean I know we talked but I can't remember what it was about, because as she was walking her hand would brush mine and I was focused at timing it right to grab it. When it happened again I held on to her hand and she stopped mid-sentence. I held my breath and she continued her story, and we walked hand-in-hand the rest of the way. I guess that was our first date," Scotty recalled. "I've never let her hand go and never will," Scotty said, glancing down at his wedding ring.

"She's an amazing kindergarten teacher, CiCi," Scotty said, suddenly feeling the need to brag on his wife a little bit. "And as much as I've learned over the years from Drew, CiCi has taught me a lot, too. She balances me completely, will call me out when I need it, but she's always my rock of support. As I worked my way up in Drew's shop, she put herself through college. She worked so hard and always pushed me to do my best. I never felt like she thought less of me for not going to college or for working for her dad," Scotty said, waiting for Paul to look his way. He did, and his guilty expression told Scotty what he already knew. Paul had always looked down on Scotty for taking a different path, and probably scheduled this fishing trip in order to boost his own ego. But this fishing trip was taking a different turn. It wasn't just about fish and being out on the water. Slowly, ideas and beliefs were being challenged and everyone was being forced to do some self-reflection and practice self-control. *It's a fishing trip Drew would have loved,* Scotty thought to himself, *but he's here in spirit, alive and well.*

"My relationship with CiCi is the one constant in my life. She knows what I'm thinking, and a lot of the time I think she wants me to succeed even more than I do. And she is her own person, which I love. She put herself through school, she found her passion and went after it. She runs marathons and volunteered at the school when Brittany was little. She's independent but completely devoted to us as a couple. She's something else..." Scotty trailed off, spinning his silver wedding band around his finger. He glanced over to Paul's hand and noticed no ring. Paul caught him looking.

"I, uhh, I take it off when I'm out of town, I mean, for fishing, ya know. Don't want it to get lost," Paul stuttered, looking half-ashamed. Scotty didn't say anything. He thought back to the ice cream date and how CiCi started showing up at the shop more often after that. He thought about picnics in the park and their first trip to the beach. He remembered losing his breath as she tossed her tank top onto the sand and rushed into the water, completely unaware of how beautiful she was. There were movie dates and phone calls that went well into the wee hours of the morning. Scotty remembered stumbling half-asleep into work the day after one of their phone call marathons, and Drew giving a short but stern reminder to not let his personal life impact his professional life.

"Sounds perfect," Paul said dryly.

"It hasn't always been great. We definitely have our ups and downs. I remember our first big fight, when CiCi was supposed to meet me after work but didn't show up. When I went to look for her, I found her at the Boys and Girls Club, surrounded by lanky, greasy-haired teenagers. Annoyed, I walked toward her, but a young guy approached her, way too handsome for my liking, and started talking to her. I remember my heart racing, my nails digging into the palms of my hands. When she laughed at something he said, I went blank. I don't remember storming up to the guy, pushing CiCi aside, and decking him in the face. I don't remember scrambling with the handsome jerk who was making her laugh, or the screams of all the bystanding kids. CiCi told me all of this later. But what I *do* remember is struggling to breathe as someone put me in a headlock, and the way my legs scraped the concrete as I was thrown out into the parking lot. When I looked up, it was Drew's disappointed face that I saw. I'll never forget it. And CiCi's heartbroken face looking out the window. I was sure I had messed up for good. I thought CiCi would never talk to me again, Drew would fire me, and the police would probably show up any minute to take me in for a battery charge or to throw me back in jail," Scotty said, still a little embarrassed by his behavior.

"I was still healing from my past; I know now that I was full of fear and it got the best of me. I had never known real love and the thought of losing it terrified me. I didn't know that at the time, but my therapist helped me realize it." Scotty laughed.

"When I calmed down, I walked home like a dog with his tail between his legs. *But who was that guy?* I would ask myself, and then get mad all over again. I was thankful my dad wasn't home when I arrived because I didn't feel like talking, and sure didn't feel like fighting. I went upstairs, took a shower, and went to sleep, sure that my life was over. All of a sudden, I felt like the punk kid again. The kid my dad said was useless. The kid with a dead mom and a mug shot. The kid who threw away every good gift he'd been given. The kid who wasn't good enough, who would never amount to anything. I told myself I was stupid for ever thinking that I could get it together, that somehow Drew could undo all of the brokenness that defined me. I remember thinking, *Well, guess I am a screwup after all, just like my dad said.*

When my alarm went off the next morning, I was tempted to hit the snooze button. But Drew's words played over and over in my head, and slowly became louder than my dad's voice.

"'You don't get to run away from this; sharks never stop moving.' So I got dressed, jumped in my car, and drove nervously toward what I assumed was my last day of work.

"When I got there, I knocked on Drew's door and he yelled for me to come in. His face was expressionless as he looked at me. He pointed to the chair. I sat. He folded his hands on his desk and looked directly into my soul. He was silent, and I knew he was waiting for me to say something. I apologized over and over again, but he was still silent. Then I realized what he was waiting for. He was waiting for me to tell him how I was going to fix it. He was waiting for my action plan, a way for me to fix what I'd done. He wasn't interested in my excuses or apologies. He was interested to see if I was going to swim forward or backward. Sharks never swim backward. When he realized what I was going to do, and that it was what he had been waiting for, I felt relieved.

"He wasn't interested in my excuses or apologies. He was interested to see if I was going to swim forward or backward."

"'I'll fix it,' I said confidently. Drew nodded and swirled his chair back around to his computer, excusing me. I grabbed my keys and headed back to my car and drove straight to the Boys and Girls Club."

"Just like that? He didn't fire you?" Zach asked in surprise.

"Nope. And he didn't say a word. He didn't have to. I had learned enough from him to know what he expected. And I knew what I had to do. I walked through the lobby and spotted the handsome jerk right away; turned out his name was Ty.

Ty with a black eye, I thought to myself, but reminded myself that this was no time for funny business. When I saw him, I contemplated walking back to my car, but I knew that my job, and any future with CiCi, probably depended on this moment. I walked up to him and tapped him on the shoulder. When he spun around and saw me, all I saw was his black eye, his tense body language, and anger rushing over his face.

"'Woah, woah. Hey, man, I'm sorry. I'm so sorry,' I said, putting my hands up as a sign of surrender. 'I messed up. I don't know what got into me. I'm really sorry about yesterday. Not cool. I lost my cool. I was wrong,' I said, my words flying out of my mouth. He looked confused and skeptical, and didn't say anything. I was waiting for him to deck me, and I knew I deserved it. I continued to defuse and deescalate the situation.

"'I just wanted to apologize. I—' "

"Why were you apologizing to this guy? He was trying to take your girl!" Zach interrupted, clearly disappointed at how Scotty handled the whole thing.

"He wasn't. I had no proof of that. They were coworkers, friends. I was in the wrong. I was being jealous and insecure and made assumptions. I was wrong," Scotty said confidently. Zach shrugged.

"After what felt like an hour of apologizing, the kid stuck out his hand to shake mine. He explained that he was recently engaged, and although CiCi was a great girl, he had no ill intentions toward her. He said we were cool, that he'd let the actions of the previous day go. He really seemed like a nice guy and I suddenly remembered sharks, that they recognize and respect other sharks. My insecurities had gotten the best of me, and I realized that there was a lot of work left to do on me.

"I went back to the shop and Drew was waiting for me. We walked into his office, he pointed to the seat, and I sat. He crossed his arms and waited for me to speak. I told him that I apologized and the guy forgave me. I explained how I was nervous at first, and then I said, 'But the thought of losing this job or CiCi motivated me to do—' and I stopped. I hadn't meant to say the part about CiCi, but Drew just raised his eyebrows. I pretended he didn't hear me.

"'Well, suckerfish, you've reminded me of the importance of humility. While you were gone I called up my brother and apologized for something I did years ago that caused us to drift apart. Today I remembered that we are never too good, too old, too experienced, too rich, or too successful to humble ourselves and admit our mistakes,' Drew told me with a gentleness.

"'Well, suckerfish, you've reminded me of the importance of humility.... Today I remembered that we are never too good, too old, too experienced, too rich, or too successful to humble ourselves and admit our mistakes."

"Man, he's a better man than me. You punch me in the face and I'd see you in court," Zach said proudly. "And you talk to my girl and you get punched in the face. You better believe you won't find me crawling back on my knees," he said with a hint of disgust in his voice, looking over at Paul for support. Previously, Zach's remarks would result in an "attaboy" or an acknowledgment from Paul, but this time, Zach's arrogant comments went ignored by his father. Paul's indifference to his comments clearly bothered Zach, who was desperately seeking his dad's approval.

Paul looked down into the bucket, where the suckerfish continued to swim around. *I can't remember the last time I apologized. To anyone,* Paul thought to himself, sitting back in his seat. *I can't remember the last time I said anything encouraging or positive about Charlotte to someone else. Or to her. I can't even think of the last time I helped someone else just to help them be successful.* Paul's stomach started to clench. He looked over at Zach. It suddenly dawned on him that Zach's attitude toward business and other people was a direct reflection of the things Paul thought, believed, and said. Paul thought, *Zach has been living inside my mouth and that's not good.* It was ugly. It was insecure. It sounded weak. Scotty was still talking, but Paul could only hear his own thoughts racing through his head. *How did I miss it all these years? I may not be the shark I thought I was. Drew sounds so cool; that is who I want to be. And Scotty's cool, too, real and transparent. This is not the same guy I grew up with. He has changed and transformed into a great man.*

He looked over at Zach. It suddenly dawned on him that Zach's attitude toward business and other people was a direct reflection of the things Paul thought, believed, and said. Paul thought, *Zach has been living inside my mouth and that's not good.*

Paul reflected on how he had thought about Scotty all these years. How he secretly loved it when people who knew him from high school would mention Scotty, and Paul would pretend to be worried about his old friend's future. He loved the part where people would compare the two of them and then make Paul out to be the success story. He remembered the way his own father had looked at him in disappointment the day Paul had come in second place at a swim meet. How the only way he could get his own dad to show up or be involved was by being the best. He loved the way his dad's eyes lit up when he told stories about stealing someone's position at work, or firing someone just to make an example out of them or to cover up his own mistake.

Paul loved swapping stories with his dad about women, and bonding over sleeping with as many as they could, like they were conquests. He thought about the seedy business deal he made that he continued to convince himself was legit. The same business decision that launched him into big boats and big paychecks and big debt. *This whole time,* Paul suddenly realized, *I've been working to get the approval of other people. My dad, girls, college professors, coaches. Scotty is not just a freakin' AC tech, and doesn't care at all about what other people think. How does he do that?* Paul thought to himself, suddenly feeling very small. *Scotty runs a $25,000,000 company!* he thought, squirming. *And if I know this, I wonder if other people can see past the big cars and boats and see who I truly am*, Paul thought, suddenly feeling exposed and embarrassed. *Heck, I financed this boat to show off,* Paul admitted to himself.

"... right, Dad?" Zach asked, pulling Paul back to the present.

"What's that, son?" Paul asked.

"Sharks don't need suckerfish. You don't have anyone latching onto you, asking for help or trying to get a free ride," Zach said, still hoping he could say something to impress his dad.

I don't have suckerfish because I'm not a shark, Paul realized, replaying the thought over and over in his head. As if in fast forward, all of Scotty's lessons played through his mind. Sharks take people with them; sharks aren't threatened by the success of others; sharks never stop swimming. *This whole time,* he thought, *I thought I was a shark.* Zach was still waiting for a response. Paul nodded, still half-dazed. Zach shrugged and went back to his phone. Scotty and Brittany were talking at the edge of the boat.

A shark recognizes another shark when they see one, Paul thought, watching Brittany and Scotty laugh together.

"So if you're not a suckerfish and you're not a shark, then what are you?" Paul finally asked, breaking the silence on the boat.

Scotty knew he had Paul right where he wanted him. *I got him. Drew taught us how to be fishers of men and this one is Moby Dick,* Scotty thought.

“If you’re not a shark, and you’re not a suckerfish,” Scotty paused for full effect, “then there is a good chance that you’re a parasite,” he said with his back toward Paul, casting a line into the water.

Paul lurched over to the side of the boat and got sick into the water.

4

Swim Lessons

Paul's sudden seasickness caught Scotty off guard, who quickly handed his rod over to Brittany and stood by Paul. Scotty knew from years of fishing that some fish vomit up their guts as you pull them out of the water. He instinctively put his hand on Paul's back to offer comfort, but the way Paul's body tensed at his touch let Scotty know that it might be better to back off. Paul reemerged, wiped the side of his mouth with his arm, and wiped his watering eyes.

"Not sure what that was about," Paul said with a small laugh, slightly embarrassed.

"Was it the motion of the boat? Or something I said?" Scotty asked, careful not to mention the P-word if that was what had caused Paul to get sick.

"No, no, it's fine. Probably something I ate this morning," he said dismissively, standing up and walking the length of the boat. "Should have taken my Dramamine," Paul mumbled. Scotty wanted to give Paul his space, so he walked toward the front of the boat. Zach picked up his phone.

"Wait, wait, wait!" Paul said excitedly. "You told us about the shark and the suckerfish, but what about the parasite? What did Drew teach you about the parasite?" he asked. Scotty noticed a sense of urgency in Paul's voice. Scotty, not surprised that Paul wanted to continue, walked back toward him and sat down.

"Parasites are nasty. Nasty, nasty. They're an entire species of microscopic nastiness. All they do is spread death and disease. This was, without a doubt, my least favorite lesson to learn. Very important, but very different from the trips to the aquarium or a day out on the boat. Are you sure you want me to..." Scotty trailed off, looking toward the water and what was left of Paul's breakfast.

"Parasites are nasty. Nasty, nasty. They're an entire species of microscopic nastiness. All they do is spread death and disease."

"Yeah, yeah, it's fine. Go ahead," Paul said, eager to leave his embarrassing moment behind them. Zach put down his phone to listen, too.

"My lesson about the parasite happened in a lab on the campus of a local college. Drew met me at the front of the shop one morning and told me we were going on a field trip. I jumped in his truck, and, like most of our other trips, we rode in silence much of the way. I always found this weird, as Drew clearly had a lot to teach me and a three-hour car ride would be the perfect place to do that. But I'd learned that sometimes silence and self-reflection taught more than asking questions and seeking answers did.

"I noticed that we began to follow signs for a prestigious college in the area; I had never stepped foot on a college campus before, and I suddenly felt uncomfortable and insecure," Scotty said.

I know the feeling, Paul thought to himself.

"It was a big campus, but Drew knew exactly where he was going, as usual. We parked in a parking garage and followed signs to the oceanography/physical sciences building. As we walked, I watched people my age, carrying books and bags and looking focused and totally in their element. They had such a different story than I did, and I was worried they could tell by looking at me that I had never even finished high school. We stopped briefly outside a multistory building, then Drew quickly and purposely took the stairs up to the main entrance. As he opened the door, the cool AC and the smell of old books hit me like a wave. The main lobby was practically empty, with just a few students huddled around a textbook at a long table by the window. Drew's steps echoed in the massive building until we stopped at an elevator. Drew hit the button and the elevator doors slid open. It was a quick trip to the third floor, and Drew made an immediate right as he stepped out of the elevator. He scanned the doors as we passed them and said 'Aha' when we reached room 308. He peered inside the rectangular window, smiled, and opened the door. An older woman looked up from her desk and peered at us over the frames of her thick glasses. She was petite, with white hair and a warm smile, like Mrs. Claus.

"'Scotty, this is Professor Carter. Professor, this is the young man I was telling you about, Scotty,' Drew said to her in a casual and familiar tone. I held out my hand to shake hers, but she got up and wrapped me in a hug instead. She smelled like peppermints.

"'So nice to meet you, Scotty! Drew's told me a lot about you. You ready to go?' she asked, looking from me and over to Drew. Drew motioned for her to lead the way and she did, taking us out of the classroom, back down the elevator and through a set of double doors that only unlocked after she used a key hanging on her necklace.

"As soon as we were through the doors, it smelled like we were in a fish market. Through large windows I could see students peering into large blue tanks, some holding clipboards and writing intently. We entered a small lab and Professor Carter flicked on the lights. I remember thinking *This must be what a morgue feels like* because it was so white, bright, sterile, and cold. She hurried around the lab with purpose, and motioned for us to follow her to a long table against the wall. There was a microscope that I was sure cost a fortune and lines of glass containers, test tubes, beakers, eye droppers, and petri dishes, all organized by size and color coded. I was careful not to touch anything. The professor sat down in front of the microscope and put her eye to the eyepiece. She adjusted a dial on the side and was quiet for a moment. She slowly lifted her head and pushed her rolling chair away from the table.

"'Now, without moving anything, come see,' she said calmly, looking at me and pointing toward the equipment. I walked toward the table and sat down, then slowly put my eye to the black plastic piece, just like she had done. I looked down the tube and let my eye focus on the tiny dots in the petri dish. 'See 'em?' she asked hopefully. I told her I just saw black dots, and she came over and adjusted the viewer. Once she did, the black dots morphed into teardrop-shaped blobs, but I still wasn't sure what I was looking at.

"'What do you notice?' she asked. *Ah, the age-old what do you notice question. Wonder if this is where Drew gets it from?* I thought to myself, looking carefully into the microscope. I explained what I saw, a small oval-shaped blob with thick lining and smaller circles inside.

"'That's a parasite,' she said, and I suddenly felt sick to my stomach. 'That tiny thing is responsible for taking down huge marine animals, like sharks and rays,' she explained. 'It's a scuticociliate, a subclass of ciliates. They're free-moving ocean organisms that operate as opportunistic parasites. They cause a common fish disease called scuticociliatosis, where tissue-eating cilia consume the blood, skin, and internal organs of their infected host,' I remember her saying, as simply and easily as if she was reading the morning paper. Drew saw the confusion in my face and laughed.

"'Professor, think you can break it down for us?' Drew asked, smiling. Professor Carter pushed a few laminated papers across the table for us to see. I immediately regretted looking at them. The highly magnified photos showed what looked like a small, hairy almond. I looked away, trying to settle my stomach.

"'They're small, but they are responsible for the downfall of animals much bigger than they are. They weasel their way in and feed off an unsuspecting shark, slowly draining its energy, health, and ability. They need the shark to survive until they drains it of all its resources, slowly contributing to its demise. It's not a mutually beneficial relationship like the one between the shark and the —'

"They're small, but they are responsible for the downfall of animals much bigger than they are. They weasel their way in and feed off an unsuspecting shark, slowly draining its energy, health, and ability."

"'Suckerfish!' I interrupted excitedly. She smiled and glanced over at Drew, who winked at her.

"'Right. The shark and the suckerfish benefit from each other, but the parasite adds no value. All a parasite does is take. Want to get another look?' she asked us, nodding toward the microscope. I put my hands up indicating I'd pass, and Drew commented that he was all too familiar with the parasite.

> "The shark and the suckerfish benefit from each other, but the parasite adds no value. All a parasite does is take."

"'Once they latch on, these little things are hard to get rid of. Once they weasel their way into the tough skin of the shark, they make themselves at home; they can even hatch their eggs inside the shark—which is why they can cause so much damage in just a short amount of time. The parasite, of course, does not have the cognitive ability to understand the damage it is doing, but even if it did, it probably wouldn't care. They're selfish little buggers, concerned only with their own survival. They have no concept of giving or providing value to the shark, and they use the shark's resources to survive. They take and give nothing in return. I know people like that, dated a few too many." She switched out the petri dish and asked me to come take another look. I should have passed. This time I didn't even need to look through the microscope to see the squiggling worm creature in the dish.

> "The parasite, of course, does not have the cognitive ability to understand the damage it is doing, but even if it did, it probably wouldn't care."

"'That's Todd. The tapeworm. You get a tapeworm when you ingest its eggs or larvae. They're a different type of parasite that affects different hosts. But their mission is the same: to use the host's resources to survive without adding any value.' She moved the petri dish from the microscope, and I was relieved when she started putting everything back in its place.

"To my horror, however, Professor Carter suggested going to lunch, and I prayed I'd be able to get the image of that hairy almond out of my head by the time we ate.

"The three of us walked the campus, passing old brick buildings, sprawling green spaces, a small pond with a dramatic water fountain. Tall oak trees created a canopy over us as we walked from the oceanography building to the library. We walked into the quiet building and headed toward the research section. Professor Carter dragged her finger down a long line of books, and stopped suddenly. She pointed to the floor, and we sat. She sat next to us and flipped through the pages until she found what she was looking for.

"'See all of these?' she asked, tapping her finger on row after row of pictures of highly magnified organisms. Some looked like the hairy almond back in the lab; others looked like worms.

"'These look more like bugs, where these guys are a type of bacteria,' she said excitedly, like she was picking out items for her Christmas list. *Nobody should be this excited about parasites,* I thought to myself, hoping this lesson would end quickly. She snapped the book shut and returned it to shelf. She explained that parasites come in all shapes and sizes, and that a lot of the time, we can be completely unaware that we have a parasite until it has already drained us of our resources and energy. 'Parasites can attack people, too,' she said, and suddenly I remembered that I needed to be much better about washing my hands with soap.

"She explained that parasites come in all shapes and sizes, and that a lot of the time, we can be completely unaware that we have a parasite until it has already drained us of our resources and energy."

"'Lunch? I'm famished,' she said with a little jump, and led us out of the library.

"We followed the professor into the on-campus pizza joint and to a booth in the back. The menus were sticky and the table hadn't been wiped down, and I wanted desperately to forget everything I had just seen and indulge in some cheesy goodness. I ran to the restroom and scrubbed down. When I returned, the professor ordered a Big Pie for the table and we sipped our sodas and talked. Professor Carter was clearly passionate about her job.

"'Did you notice the tiny hairlike membranes on the outside of the specimen we looked at back at the lab? Those help the parasite navigate through the shark's nose and up into its brain. There, it slowly begins to eat away at the muscle, causing the shark to become incapacitated and disoriented. Usually, this means they lose the ability to swim and they die, or they beach themselves by accident. It's truly a sad sight to see. This huge powerful creature can be taken down by this little tiny parasite. But more research needs to be done to learn more. It's all in the initial stages right now," she said, lifting a greasy piece of pizza to her mouth. I was silent until a not-so-subtle kick to my shin prompted me to speak up.

"'Oh, fascinating, for sure,' I blurted. I asked for a to-go box for my slices. As always, Drew picked up the tab, and we walked out toward the center of campus.

"'We should be heading back now, don't want to get home too late,' Drew said after a few moments.

"'Okay, Andrew, that's fine,' she smiled. 'It was so nice to meet you, Scotty,' she said, wrapping me in another hug. 'If you ever want to come and help with my parasite research, you're more than welcome!' she teased as she rubbed my back. I thanked her and stepped back to let Drew say his goodbyes.

She whispered something to him as they hugged and I looked away, letting them have their moment. But what I heard next caused me to snap my head back in their direction so fast that I almost broke my neck.

"'Love you, too, Mom, call you later,' Drew said, pulling away from her embrace. He noticed the shock on my face and looked pleased. He thrived on surprises and catching people off guard. Professor Carter was already walking back to her lab, and we set out to the truck."

"Wait, wait," Paul interrupted. "Drew's mom was the *fish teacher*?" he exclaimed.

Scotty smiled and nodded. "I was surprised, too. She insisted on calling him Andrew. In fact, come to find out, she hates when people call him Drew. Drew talked all about her on the way home, how she raised four boys on her own, how she worked three jobs to make ends meet but still made it to all of their activities and sporting events. They had a little house in Lazy Lake, and she expected Drew and his three brothers to pitch in from an early age to keep it looking tidy and neat. They rotated chores, one doing the lawn, one doing the kitchen and bathrooms, one making the beds, and one doing laundry. She brought them to church every Sunday, and they stayed after to help clean up when everyone else headed to get breakfast. They tagged along with her to the local soup kitchen to serve the homeless, and they helped her babysit for the teen mom down the street. Giving and serving is in their DNA. She loved the ocean and saved up every year to take the boys to a cheap motel on the water, where she built sandcastles with them and pointed out different sea creatures and birds. She'd splurge on ice cream cones for all of them, and then fall asleep in the armchair as she sang to all four of them, tucked in to the two queen-size beds. Made me miss my mom so bad. I could see where Drew got his love for family and serving others from. I could see why it was so important to raise his kids right, to pass down the important stuff, to keep his mom's legacy alive. I could see why he put so much effort in teaching people, and in paying close attention to the way his words and actions impacted others."

"So how'd she end up as a professor?" Zach asked.

"She took a class or two at the local college when Drew and his brothers were little. Sometimes she'd have to take a year off, sometimes she was lucky and could afford two classes in a semester. It was a quiet, private, personal thing. She'd put her boys and her community first, but she had this goal of teaching oceanography at the college level, and she persisted. Drew told me about finding her asleep with her head on the kitchen table, surrounded by textbooks. When he gently woke her, she sprang to her feet to get her small army out the door. It took years, but she finally did it—she earned her degree and started teaching the Oceanography 101 course at the local college. She eventually moved up to the university level and has been there ever since. She was serious about reaching her goal, but she was more serious about making sure she raised four kind, honest, reliable, productive, giving, humble, and hardworking men," Scotty said, and realized that the more he remembered Professor Carter, the more it sounded like he was talking about CiCi. He played with his wedding ring and was suddenly anxious to get home to her.

Paul looked over at Zach. All this talk about great mothers made him think of his own mom. The woman who pushed herself to be perfect to meet the impossible expectations of a man, Paul's father, who would never be satisfied. The beautiful woman who never felt good enough, pretty enough, smart enough. The young mom who let go of her dreams and ambitions to be a trophy wife of someone who didn't even know she had dreams. And he suddenly felt sad for her, realizing that although she was known for hosting the best block parties and running in elite social circles, she must have felt so alone. Paul's stomach tightened as his brain made the connection between his mother and the woman he married. Junie. The sweet girl with so much potential who wanted to be loved and wanted so hard to make it work with the quarterback who stole her virginity way before prom night. The girl who moved mountains for his happiness and gave up searching for her own. And he never even noticed or cared. He remembered the jealousy he felt as she stared into their newborn baby's eyes, and wondered why she never smiled at him like that. She was a fantastic mother, and Zach loved her. Truly loved her. She wanted so badly for her son to have a life where he felt seen and appreciated while being grounded and confident. Paul wasn't sure how to do the dad thing, so he compensated with toys and gadgets and gifts.

And when Junie began to put her foot down, demanding that her son have a life full of love and experiences instead of new bikes and toys, Paul panicked. The combination of seeing the way she wholeheartedly adored him, along with the pressure to give his son something he didn't have, was all it took for him to distance himself. Work trips got longer, phone calls became less frequent, fights got more intense. Paul knew Junie would continue to try to make it work, but Paul knew he'd fail. So when a woman in a red dress and black heels approached him at the networking event, he made a call to Junie that the meeting got extended and he'd be home in a few days. Being tangled up with Charlotte in the penthouse suite for the weekend felt like an escape for Paul, a chance to finally breathe and do something right for a change. When Junie found the hotel receipt, Paul knew it was over because June wouldn't ever turn a blind eye to anything. She would confront him and always hold him accountable. When it was finally over, a part of him was relieved. She took Zach and moved into a cute bungalow near the water that Paul felt very generous paying for.

The best decision I ever made was picking the right mom for my kid, Paul thought. *She wasn't the right wife for me. Or maybe I wasn't the right husband for her. To her. But Zach got an incredible mother out of what I assumed was a mistake, . . .* he thought.

Paul made it to most birthday parties, and would surprise Zach with a big check in the mail every once in a while. He always meant to call and get together with his growing son, but deals had to be made and work had to be done and he kept putting it off. It was only a few months after Zach turned 18 that Zach showed up at Paul's front door demanding answers. They started going out on the boat, racing fast cars, taking impromptu trips to Paris. Paul had hoped that the trips and the gifts were enough to make up for his years of absence, but he knew deep down that they weren't. The way that Zach still constantly sought his father's approval felt all too familiar. When Paul thought about it, he didn't really know his son. He didn't know what he was afraid of, or what he wanted to be as an adult, or if he had even been heartbroken. Paul felt a lump in his throat as he watched Scotty engage in conversation with Zach. Zach looked so interested in what Scotty was saying, and Paul noticed the way Scotty listened, really listened, to what Zach was saying.

Paul got lost in thought again, thinking of how Drew talked about his mom and Scotty talked about CiCi, and realized that in the short time that Zach and Paul had reconnected, all Paul had done was bash Junie. But she was the one reason Zach was still a decent kid, and Paul could see how he was already messing it up. Junie was selfless and serving, and Zach was too. But recently, Paul noticed Zach's more selfish tendencies and foolishly saw them as showing that his son was a chip off the old block. Zach was watching Paul toss people aside to get where he needed to go, and was slowly starting to do the same. *His comments today about the shark and the suckerfish, they were all me. They were all things I've said, or would say, and be proud of,* Paul thought, feeling like he would be sick again. *We're all in charge of leaving a legacy, and I'm not so sure I'm leaving the right one.*

"So what did she teach you about the parasites?" Zach asked, bringing Paul back to the present.

"Well, thankfully we didn't have to get up close and personal with any other nasty parasites; that part of our lesson was over. But to be honest, there's no great way to learn about parasites. They're just naturally disgusting." Scotty laughed. *And when people act like parasites, that's even worse,* he thought.

"There's no great way to learn about parasites. They're just naturally disgusting." Scotty laughed. *And when people act like parasites, that's even worse,* he thought.

"Drew used our ride back home to help connect what we had learned at the university with what he wanted me to learn. A parasite is anyone in your life who takes from you but does not add value. They are not interested in using their strengths to benefit you; they are solely interested in their own survival, even if it means causing damage to you or others. And they can be hard to get rid of. Parasites know that their best chance of survival is finding a host to attach to, and once they get settled, they get to work in bringing the host down. I remember thinking, *Sounds a lot like my dad*, but I must have said it out loud, because Drew said, 'Mine too.'

"A parasite is anyone in your life who takes from you but does not add value."

"It was quiet for a while as I thought about my dad, and I realized that ever since I had saved up enough to rent to move into the studio apartment next to the shop, I hadn't heard from him. The last time I had seen him was when I was packing up the few things I had and loading them into my truck. He had come out to the driveway, and I could smell the alcohol as he approached. I remember being shocked at how old and sad he looked. He put his hand on my back and slurred something about how I was leaving my old man behind. Abandoning him, just like my you-know-what of a mother had done, he slurred. He put both hands on the car to hold himself up and I was so relieved to go and never look back.

"'I'm gonna go now, Pops. I'll see you later,' I said, shutting the trunk.

"'Don't worry about coming back. You go fix heaters or whatever it is you do. Too bad you couldn't be a lawyer like I was. Druggie. That's what time jail … time … jail time will do. Too bad,' he said, trying to sound mean but sounding stupid instead. I wanted so bad to punch him, to tell him what a waste of space he was and that he hadn't deserved Mom. But I pushed past him, got in my truck, and peeled away. I didn't even look back. Literally. I didn't even look in the rearview mirror. I just left.

"'But there's something you need to know about parasites,' Drew said, pulling me back to the present. 'There's hope for them. People who are parasites in your life are not bound to be parasites forever. They, unlike the ocean species, are capable of thought and reason and education and change. Same goes for sharks and suckerfish. Just because you're one now doesn't mean you'll be one forever. It's all very fluid and should be evaluated on a case-by-case basis.

> "People who are parasites in your life are not bound to be parasites forever.... It's all very fluid and should be evaluated on a case-by-case basis.... In some of your relationships you'll be the shark and in some you'll be the suckerfish."

"'In some of your relationships you'll be the shark and in some you'll be the suckerfish. It all depends on the person you are connecting with. But nobody should be a parasite. If a suckerfish gets mentored the right way by a shark, eventually it will become a shark, too. Sharks can have parasitic tendencies sometimes, but they are quick to notice them and make changes. Don't think that all sharks are buddy-buddy with suckerfish—some sharks even eat suckerfish and don't take them for a ride or work in tandem. The business world is full of sharks who only look out for themselves and could care less about others' success.'

> "If a suckerfish gets mentored the right way by a shark, eventually it will become a shark, too."

"When I think about Drew, I think of him as a gigantic great white. A great white shark can have thirty suckerfish connected to it all at the same time. That's the goal of the Sacred Six; we all should aspire to become great whites.

> "A great white shark can have thirty suckerfish connected to it all at the same time. That's the goal of the Sacred Six; we all should aspire to become great whites."

"'Parasites have a harder time making the shift at first, but they can do it,' Drew told me. I felt defensive, angry that anyone would assume that a parasite like my dad could be anything else than a cold-hearted, selfish, waste of a life. Maybe some parasites were capable of reconciliation, but my dad was the worst of the worst, and I hated even letting him take up space in my brain. But I realized as I matured that my dad was a broken man and that he was no different than the boys at the shop. The only difference was that they had met Drew.

"My dad never had a good role model, a good mentor. That's why mentorship is so important to me. It changed my life, so I am committed to change others' lives. We all need support; we all need great leadership and great mentors. We all need to get connected to the right sharks at some point in our life, and we all need to be suckerfish before we can ever become good sharks. You first need to become a great follower of someone else's vision before you are fully prepared to follow your own. Make sense? I think some people think they are sharks, but are really just huge, giant parasites. Tough to tell 'em apart, to be honest, especially the ones with money.

"We all need support; we all need great leadership and great mentors. We all need to get connected to the right sharks at some point in our life, and we all need to be suckerfish before we can ever become good sharks. You first need to become a great follower of someone else's vision before you are fully prepared to follow your own."

Paul looked out over the water. Scotty noticed Brittany quietly revel in Paul's silence. They hadn't thrown a line into the water for over an hour, but Paul suddenly had the urge to break away from the conversation and put some bait on his line. He sent his line out into the water and watched the bobber bounce on the water while he thought. He had always assumed that the tough love and hard lessons he had learned from his dad were what enabled him to be so successful. Paul thought back to a vivid memory of his dad belittling a waitress at a restaurant they used to go to, complaining about everything from the food to her ability to write down their order. Visibly flustered, she had gotten a manager, who had taken care of the whole meal, and Paul's dad had been so proud. *I was so proud of him in the moment,* Paul thought, *because he was so proud of himself. He felt big and powerful, and I saw him as big and powerful. My dad, the guy who got stuff done. But he did it by embarrassing that waitress and didn't feel bad about it,* Paul thought, his stomach turning. This memory started a train of memories of times Paul did the same thing. He thought about his habit of finding a small flaw in a business deal or a dinner Charlotte had made and using it as a way to get loud and boisterous and feel important. Suddenly he felt small and wanted to be anywhere but this boat, where he felt exposed and embarrassed.

Paul thought back to the years he spent trying to impress his dad—on the swim team, in school, with the ladies, on the football field. Paul spent so much energy trying to measure up, and his dad was relentless in tearing him down. *Hard to get rid of,* Paul thought, thinking about what Scotty had said about parasites being stubborn and hard to get rid of. Even when Paul moved out, his father's voice was there, reminding him of how he wasn't quite good enough. The example that his father had set for him was so engrained in who Paul was that he began to worry that these traits would be hard, if not impossible, to get rid of. *They take and take but never give,* Paul thought. At first, he didn't think this really applied to his own dad, since his dad had provided a great house and family vacations for the family, and had given Paul had a brand-new car when he turned 16.

But when he tried to think of a time his dad gave him a compliment, gave him a chance, gave him grace, gave him wisdom, gave him time, he came up empty. When Paul began to think of the things his father took from him—confidence, time, knowledge, a peaceful childhood—he got angry.

What am I taking from Zach? What have I taken from Junie and Charlotte? What have I taken from the people in my company? And aside from money, what have I given them? Paul wondered, almost frantically. He searched his brain for answers. *Surely I must have mentored someone? Who have I mentored, impacted, or help make successful?* Paul thought. *Is there anyone in my life who talks about me the way Scotty talks about Drew?*

"That night, as we were closing up, Drew asked me what I remembered about our quick pop into the library. I remembered the professor showing us different types of parasites, and mentioning that they all look different and cause different types of damage. He nodded, and went on to explain that sometimes the parasites in our lives aren't our overly critical bosses or our deadbeat dads. They can be well-meaning friends and family members who are unaware of their effect on those around them. Or perhaps they are aware, but don't know how to change it. Although in the ocean the suckerfish devours any parasite they see, it doesn't work like that in the real world. Sometimes we can't simply dismiss or destroy the parasites in our lives. Instead, we can have a greater impact by helping them see the way that their actions affect others, and offer patience and grace in their journey toward transformation. And if they clearly see the error of their ways and choose to continue the behavior, well, that's another ball game altogether."

"Then you destroy them!" Zach said eagerly.

Scotty smiled. "Not quite, but you make intentional efforts to prevent them from taking one more minute of your time or one more ounce of your energy. And if they come around, and they show proof that they've changed their ways, or at least a willingness to learn how —"

"You tell 'em too bad, so sad," Zach said, like an evil villain from a movie.

"You offer grace and you give them a second chance, because we can all become a parasite, if only for a moment, when we're selfish," Scotty corrected. Zach sighed in defeat. "I mean, if you think about it, Drew created an environment where he welcomed broken kids who were takers, parasites of sorts, but he transformed us into suckerfish and eventually into sharks. We are all sharks. During my most miserable days, I was always focused on me only. Drew taught me to come alive by managing how I operate and how I manage relationships. The shark, the suckerfish, and the parasite represent three types of people who can make or break your life," Scotty said with passion.

"Drew created an environment where he welcomed broken kids who were takers, parasites of sorts, but he transformed us into suckerfish and eventually into sharks.... The shark, the suckerfish, and the parasite represent three types of people who can make or break your life."

Paul's brain felt like it was in overdrive, like he was dreaming. He felt like everything he had believed about himself, his family, his marriage, and Scotty was all wrong. He had scheduled this trip with a subconscious desire to check in on his "troubled" friend and compare his own success to Scotty's. He had done it to show off his new boat, to make sure Scotty knew how successful he was. But now, in just a few short hours, everything had been turned upside down. He came on the boat feeling like a shark, a powerful and successful businessman who never took no for an answer, raising his son as another ruthless shark to continue his legacy. He came on the boat with the idea that Scotty was less capable, less successful, and less powerful than he was, that he was the victim of a lifetime of bad choices that led him to a mediocre life. But now, it was different. Paul did not feel like a shark. He felt exposed and small and embarrassed. He felt unsure of where he fit in the dynamic of the boat, and the dynamic of every other relationship in his life. His indifference toward others was not alpha, it was parasitic. His relentless forward movement in pursuit of success, regardless of the wake of disaster he left behind, was not that of a shark, but of a selfish parasite with no concern for others. Everything he did that he thought made him look intimidating, formidable, and powerful was actually flashing signs of his incompetence and insecurity. *But there is hope for the parasite,* Paul heard himself whisper. *Who I am now, who I have always been, is not who I have to be,* he thought, feeling a slight sense of relief.

Paul did not feel like a shark. He felt exposed and small and embarrassed.... *Who I am now, who I have always been, is not who I have to be,* he thought.

"As I helped Drew close up the shop that night, I saw a shadowy figure approach the shop. Mako growled, and I was once again thankful for his protection.

"'Hey, Drew?' I asked, slightly nervous as the tall figure got closer to the front door. Drew didn't respond, and I stayed tucked away, watching to see what the stranger did next. He came right up to the front door and knocked. He called out for Drew, which made me feel a little better, and then reached for the door knob. He twisted the knob and poked his head in and called for Drew again.

"'Can I help you?' I asked, pushing my chest out a little, walking with confidence.

"'Uh yeah, hi, is Drew here?' he asked, looking around, looking nervous. Mako stood in between me and the stranger, a low growl rumbling in his throat.

"'Who are you?' I asked, a little more aggressively than I meant to.

"'Is Drew here?' the guy asked again. I took a step toward him and asked again, 'Who are you? What do you need?' We all were protective of our shark. Before the stranger could answer, Drew appeared from the back.

"'Ah, Jim. You're here. Okay. Sorry, we can clean up and get out of here,' Drew said, lacking the usual assurance in his voice. Jim stepped aside and avoided eye contact with me, but I stared right through him. We followed Drew out in silence; when Drew locked the door, I noticed his hands were shaking.

"'See you tomorrow, Scotty,' Drew waved to me, but he didn't move. The guy stood with his arms crossed across his chest, watching me. It was clear that Drew didn't want me to go, but I suddenly felt unsure. He waved me away again, with a little more persistence this time, so I got in my truck and pulled away. As I looked in my rearview mirror, I saw the two guys shaking hands before I turned the corner and they were out of sight.

"The next day, I got to the shop early, hoping to catch Drew before the 8 a.m. meeting and get the details on this random guy who had showed up the night before. The door was open, and when I peeked in I saw Drew sitting at his desk, so I half knocked and entered at the same time. I stopped in my tracks when I saw the stranger, Jim, sitting in the seat in the corner of the room, half hidden by the filing cabinet.

"'Oh. Sorry, I didn't... I uhh, I'll come back,' I said, backing out of the room with my hands up.

"'No, no, it's okay. Come in, Scotty," Drew said as he motioned me into the room. I stood in the doorway, avoiding eye contact with Jim.

"'This is Jim. We knew each other a long time ago. We haven't . . . he and I . . . we just recently reconnected,' Drew said, and I could tell he was being selective with his words. I nodded in acknowledgment at Jim, but he just stared at me. I disliked this guy already. Drew could probably see the confusion on my face, so he politely dismissed me, supposedly so they could wrap things up, but probably so I didn't ask any questions or make things weird.

"A little while later, Drew walked Jim through the shop and out the front door. Drew reappeared, didn't say a word, went into his office, and closed the door. At 8:05 when he didn't open up for the morning meeting, I took it upon myself to lead the meeting and get the day started. We didn't see much of Drew for the rest of the day. All day I was thinking, *What the heck? Something ain't right. I can feel it.*

"Right at noon, CiCi surprised me with a picnic lunch wearing a sundress and suggested we head down to the water for lunch. The look in her eyes was flirtatious, and I had never cleaned up my station so fast in my life. We walked hand-in-hand toward the water and claimed a spot under a large tree. She laid out the blanket and I unpacked the basket and got us all settled. We . . . uhh . . ." Scotty stopped, remembering who was listening to his story.

"We did a little cuddling . . . ," he started, looking over at Brittany. She rolled her eyes and smiled.

"Anyway, she was laying there, her head on my chest, and I was playing with her hair. She asked about how my day was going, and I always loved how I could tell she was really listening. 'And then the weird guy from last night was in your dad's office this morning. Weird guy. I don't like him,' I told her.

"'Who? What guy?' she asked, sipping her lemonade.

"'I don't know. He showed up last night and your dad kind of sent me away. He was there this morning. Jim? I don't —" But I couldn't finish because CiCi sat up so fast I thought a bug had bit her.

"'Who did you say?' she asked, more serious than I had ever seen her.

"'I… his name was Jim, I think. What?' I asked, confused at her reaction. "'Tall, skinny, shady looking?' I said, searching her face for a reaction. She was still staring me down, not saying anything. "'Babe? What? Who is it? Drew said he knew him from a long time ago?' I asked, concerned. I put my hand on hers and she yanked it away.

"'I have to go. Can you?' she asked, motioning toward the picnic.

"'Yeah, of course, I mean, but why?' I asked, but she was already running toward the shop. I shoved everything in the basket and followed after her. I got to the shop just in time to see her swing open the shop door and disappear inside. I could hear her yelling from the shop.

"'Why was he here?' she yelled, and I could tell in her voice that she was crying. It took everything in me not to fly in there and scoop her up. I waited.

"'CiCi, honey, calm down. I was going to tell you. It's all news to me, too,' Drew said, putting his hands up in surrender.

"'You brought him *here*?' she said, calmly and slowly.

"'I. Yes. He wanted to talk and I thought I would give him the chance to tell his side of the story and—'

"'What side of the story? What else do you need to know? He drove drunk and he KILLED MY BROTHER! What are we going to do next, sit down and have a beer with him? I am an only child because of him!' she roared. Drew was silent. 'Mom was never the same because of him! When he killed the baby he killed a part of her, too!' she shouted, and then stood there, waiting for an answer. Before anyone could say anything else, she turned around to run out of the office but ran into me instead. She collapsed into me, and I have never wanted to protect someone so much in my life. I looked at Drew as I stroked her hair and he rubbed his beard with his fingers.

"'Get me out of here,' CiCi whispered into my chest. I grabbed her hand and we walked out of the shop. I waited for Drew to call me to come back, but he didn't, so we got in my truck and headed to the beach.

"Turns out, this Jim guy left a bar one afternoon, drunk out of his mind. Got on the highway in Boca Raton and somehow found himself in Broward. CiCi's mom was picking up CiCi's brother from daycare. This was before CiCi was born. The baby died on impact, and her mom never really got through it—I mean of course, I can't even imagine," Scotty said quietly, looking over at Brittany. The boat was silent. "CiCi's mom was a sweet lady, loved her family, but she was sad a lot, often kept to herself. Drew didn't say much about it, but did mention that the loss of their son sent Deb, his wife, into a dark cloud of depression. She blamed herself for the accident. Even though CiCi didn't know the baby, she mourned for her mom, who died emotionally in that accident. She hated watching Deb sob on the baby's birthday or disappear for days on the anniversary of the accident. CiCi hated Jim for breaking her mother's heart. Her spirit," Scotty said in a quiet tone. "It was Drew's job to run the shop, it was her job to manage the home. Drew could never cheer Deb up, so he found his joy and healing at work."

"So why was this guy in the shop? How could Drew even be in the same room as this guy?" Paul asked.

"Apparently the guy did his time, became a model prisoner, really turned his life around. Went to AA in jail and out. Part of his treatment was seeking forgiveness from the people he hurt. So he had reached out to Drew and Drew agreed to meet him—you know the guy Drew was. Second chances and all of that." Scotty shrugged. It was who he was; he was a great man with a great heart and couldn't hold a grudge if he tried.

"That night when he came to the shop was the first time Drew had seen the guy since the day of the trial. Drew never talked about their conversation or what was discussed. Eventually, years later, CiCi agreed to talk to Jim and he apologized. She let him have it, though. She let him know exactly what she thought of him, and I sat by her the whole time, holding her hand. He let her go on and on, took it all, all the name calling and anger, and just took it. I could see the remorse in his face, and for a split second I saw him as a human instead of a monster. And then I saw him as a version of me, a very likely version of me if I hadn't been scooped up by Drew. I could have just as likely had too much to drink and made a stupid decision and ruined my life or took someone else's. *That could have been me*, I thought to myself, *that would have been me.* CiCi said what she had to say, listened to his apology, and we left. It would be years before she told him that she forgave him. That accident impacted CiCi's relationship with her mom. That's why CiCi is so passionate and why she and Brittany are so close.

"Mrs. Peters never got there, could never bring herself to come face-to-face with Jim. Even on Sundays at church, when the pastor talked about forgiveness, Deb would leave the sanctuary and sit in the car. Drew would try to get Deb to recite the Sacred Six but she refused. 'Sharks always look up and never look down,' Drew would say. Deb believed that her anger would keep her son's spirit alive, but it slowly drained her. It was like sadness, bitterness, and anger had latched on to her like parasites and had laid eggs for years.

"This was the first time I completely understood what Drew meant when he talked about there being hope for the parasite. Someone is not destined to be a parasite forever—in fact people can be very selfish all the time or just sometimes. Unlike the nasty ocean organisms, people who are parasites can change, improve, even thrive. Jim was selfish and not concerned with the well-being of others in that stage of his life. He was broken and rough and left a trail of death and destruction everywhere he went. It may have taken a third of his life in jail to break through it, but he did it. He was surrounded by people who made bad decisions and instead of falling into that life, he sought out people who could give him the best chance of success. The people he could follow and trust. I mean if you think about it, Drew transformed me from a parasite to a suckerfish to now, well—"

"A shark," Paul interrupted, finally turning to look at Scotty with validation. "Sharks don't just swim, they SWIM. Sharks don't operate like other fish. Jim got connected to a shark someplace," Paul said in careful realization.

"Sharks don't just swim, they SWIM."

"Yeah, even in jail, there are sharks. People with a purpose and an others-focused attitude, truly remorseful and rehabilitated. And in prison he found mentors and Jim attached himself to them like a—"

"Suckerfish," Paul said, the concept making his head spin.

"Right," Scotty smiled. "Even in the darkest places, in the worst situations, in the aftermath of the worst you've ever been, you can find a shark. Sharks are everywhere; you just have to find them. And when you do, and you're committed to the mutually beneficial relationship, you can radically change the trajectory of your life. Jim will always be the one who killed CiCi's brother. He will always have to check the yes box for the 'Have you ever committed a felony?' question when filling out paperwork. There are lifelong consequences for his stupid decision that day, but that decision does not have to define him.

"Sharks are everywhere; you just have to find them. And when you do, and you're committed to the mutually beneficial relationship, you can radically change the trajectory of your life."

"His past, his selfishness, the way he treated others, and his mistakes do not secure him a spot in the parasite category for life. In AA, he is surrounded by sharks and suckerfish. He is taking his role as a suckerfish seriously, understanding the power of mentorship, and moving forward from his mistakes. Drew told me something about Jim that really stuck with me. He said, 'It is not your past decisions that define you, it is your next one.' This experience helped me understand the way a parasite can quickly take down the people around it, but also that it is not a life sentence if you choose change."

"It is not your past decisions that define you, it is your next one."

Scotty was still impressed by how a tiny microscopic organism can teach someone so much about life and choices and hope. At this point, everyone was engaged in the story and Paul's bobber danced slowly in the water, ignored.

"I have two questions, Scotty," Paul stated. "First question: Who was Drew's shark?"

"Easy. His mom, Professor Carter. She taught him everything. Her husband—his dad, 'the parasite'—he was a womanizer and a smooth talker; when he took off, the first thing she did was go back to her maiden name. She didn't want any affiliation with that sleaze bucket. She was left to fend for herself with her four boys. By going to the ocean with his mom and brothers, Drew developed a fondness for the ecosystem of the ocean and for sharks especially. In fact, the Sacred Six was based on many things his mom would say. Drew's mom was the catalyst for the Sacred Six."

"Second question," Paul began. "Earlier you said that there is hope for the parasite. How does that work? How does someone so self-involved change their ways and rid themselves of that title?"

"Yes. There's hope for the parasite. Like Jim, parasites just need to be shown how their attitude and their actions impact others. They need to be open to constructive criticism and be willing to make changes. Some parasites know that's what they are and are fine with it. They have no intention of changing or bettering themselves or their company. HR departments know their parasites: they don't work hard, they don't impact the culture, and they complain and bring negative energy daily. Then they can hide behind unions and make false claims of harassment or racism or sexism. These things can happen, but a parasite can stir the pot with the best of them. When the leader is a parasite, that's different ball game. The culture is horrible. There is no hope for someone who does not want to change and have a positive impact. Hope and change start with an acknowledgment of weakness and an open-mindedness to making hard choices that will lead to a happier, healthier, and more productive life. Make sense?" Scotty asked.

Paul processed the information, and nodded.

> "Parasites just need to be shown how their attitude and their actions impact others.... Some parasites know that's what they are and are fine with it. They have no intention of changing or bettering themselves or their company."

"Everyone ready to head back?" Scotty asked, suddenly feeling very tired. This day of fishing had turned into something much more than what he had expected. The way Paul and Zach were engaged in the story made Scotty feel that maybe, just maybe, they had absorbed some of the information and that Drew was still teaching his lessons from the grave.

Paul watched as Zach looked out over the water. He wondered if anything Scotty had said had moved him. He studied his son's face, but could not tell whether he was deep in self-reflection or just anxious to get back to a place where he could charge his phone. He thought about Jim and how he had turned his life around, and wondered whether, if a drunk driver could turn his life around, maybe an absent, self-centered dad could do the same. He wondered if Zach had heard the stories about parasites and immediately thought of his old man. The thought made him cringe. *But even worse, what if he doesn't see it at all?* Paul thought. *What if, after all of this, Zach does not see that his mindset, the mindset that I've taught him, is self-fulfilling and misguided? What if he believes that his "me-focused" attitude is a sign of strength instead of an insecurity?* Paul felt anxious, wanting to grab his son and undo all the damage, but wasn't sure how. He felt helpless. He wasn't sure he would be able to undo the toxic masculinity and selfish attitude he'd been so proud of just hours ago. This fishing trip had turned into a life-changing seminar.

Zach looked out over the water. He could feel his dad staring at him, but couldn't bring himself to make eye contact. This was supposed to be a boring fishing trip with people he barely knew and a half-assed attempt at quality time with his dad. This wasn't what he signed up for. He didn't sign up for all of these stories and self-reflection. He wondered if his dad could see himself in any of the stories that Scotty told, or if he was too self-absorbed to even see that Scotty was practically describing him to a T. *I learned some stuff today my dad never taught me. It felt good, too, it felt right,* Zach thought to himself. *Dad is just like grandpa. And if I'm not careful, I could end up like both of them. I mean, they're not horrible people, but there are some things I know need to change,* he thought to himself.

Zach wanted so badly to have his dad listen to him like Scotty did. He wanted his dad to ask him questions, to show him how to build a business with integrity, how to fall in love instead of just falling into bed with the first woman in a red dress and heels that approached him. He regretted the way he would dismiss his mother as soon as his dad popped into the picture. He reached for his phone to text her, but remembered that he needed to charge his phone. *I don't care if he sees it or not. I'm not going to be a damn parasite,* Zach thought, feeling angry and determined and confused all at the same time. *I don't know if my dad took any of this in, but I see it. And if Jim can turn his life around, I can, too. And Dad can, too. I just have to figure out how,* he thought, feeling a little more confident. He finally turned and met his dad's stare. Zach wasn't sure, because he had never seen it before, but something was different about his dad's eyes. They looked glassy, almost watery. The sight immediately made his eyes burn, so he looked back over the water. *Maybe he got it,* Zach thought, and felt himself smiling.

Paul broke the loud silence. "Ya know, I get Drew now. I totally get Drew now. Here is a guy who never really knew his dad, and lost his son, too. Talk about feeling empty. He must have hurt inside and felt a void, so he did need suckerfish.

Maybe consciously he didn't even know he needed a suckerfish; he just knew he needed to fill that void. You and the other AC techs became like the sons he never had, and he wanted to give you guys the dad you never had. That's why being a great father and mentor was so important to Drew. In fact, Scotty, I feel like I can really see where Drew was coming from, understand his heart. And, on behalf of Drew, I do think it is safe to say you were the special son he never had. I'm confident Drew is in heaven and so proud of you. You are carrying on his legacy of the Sacred Six," Paul said, putting his arm around Scotty's shoulders. "In just a few hours, you have changed my life, Scotty. I mean it. And I am proud of you too, my man," Paul said, wrapping Scotty in a hug.

Brittany watched in amazement as the two men hugged. Her annoyance and frustration subsided, and her heart instantly softened toward the big, arrogant jerk. She suddenly saw Paul differently, his transparency instantly touching her heart. She saw the small damaged boy on the inside of him, desperate for attention and validation. She stood up and joined in on the hug. Scotty just blushed with pride. Zach thought about it, but decided to watch from afar instead, still cautious and confused.

5

FLIP FLOP

Scotty looked around the boat, touched by the day's events but even more so by Paul's comments. He couldn't believe what he had just heard. Everyone seemed to be in a state of shock and silent self-reflection. The only sound was the humming of the engine as the boat cut through the waves. When Scotty had packed up for this trip this morning, he had thought about the best-case scenario and the worst-case scenario. The best: Paul would be a completely changed person from high school, be a joy to hang out with, and this trip would be the start of rekindling an old friendship. The worst: He'd be exactly the same as he had been and it would be the worst day in fishing history. But this trip was turning out to be dramatically different than Scotty had expected. The best and the worst cases both had happened on the same day. Paul wouldn't leave as the same man he had been when he boarded.

Scotty noticed that Brittany was tracing the outline of her shark tooth necklace, which meant that whatever thoughts were running through her mind were bothering her. Scotty figured she felt bad about being judgmental and a little too tough on Paul. Brittany and her mom struggled with their emotions from time to time, and she knew it.

Scotty realized he hadn't checked his phone all day, which he often saw as a good sign that he was being intentional and productive. He had a missed text from CiCi asking how the trip was going, but what stopped him in his tracks was seeing the date. His stomach dropped for a second, and then he smiled. *Tomorrow is Drew's birthday,* Scotty thought, and took a deep breath. How perfect, how coincidental, how crazy was it that he was here, in the middle of the ocean, teaching Drew's lessons the day before his birthday? He suddenly felt bad for leaving CiCi at home, and wanted to get back to her to hold her. *Tomorrow is going to be rough for her; it's rough for all of us*, he thought. He tucked his phone back in his pocket and looked out over the water. "It's Drew's birthday tomorrow," he said out loud. He heard Brittany gasp. She covered her mouth with her hands and Scotty noticed the sadness in her eyes.

"I can't believe I forgot!" she said, clearly feeling guilty.

"You didn't forget. It's tomorrow. We're good," he said, putting his hand on her shoulder.

"We need to get back home to Mom," she said quietly. Scotty squeezed her shoulder and nodded.

"That means tomorrow is also the anniversary of another big milestone," Scotty smiled. "CiCi and I had been dating for almost three years, and I knew she was it for me almost from day one. I had known the moment I punched the guy in the face at the Boys and Girls Club. Or the day after my adventure through the woods. I knew by the way my heart skipped every time she showed up for lunch, and how it sank when she didn't come. As I learned more and more about what it meant to be a shark, I found myself wanting to be a shark not just for me, but for *her.* To be the one who added value to *her* life, who took her where I was going, who fought for her, supported her, and gave her everything I had because she gave me so much.

"CiCi had mentioned that she was going last-minute shopping with her mom for a birthday present for her dad, so I knew that I had a small window of time to head over to Drew's house and have the conversation. I traded my ripped jeans for the one pair of khakis that I owned and found a navy blue polo tucked in the back of the closet. I practiced what I was going to say the entire drive over, and took a deep breath as I got out of the car. The grandeur of the large estate never ceased to impress me: the gorgeous arches and columns, the sweeping front porch, the large windows, the perfectly landscaped yard. I wiped my sweaty palms on my pants and knocked on the door. Drew opened the door and wrapped me in a hug, welcoming me into the living area.

"'A birthday surprise!' Drew smiled, motioning for me to take a seat. I immediately felt foolish for not showing up with a gift. Drew fell into his favorite leather recliner, muted the TV, and swiveled to face me.

"'What's going on?' Drew asked with a smile. 'Just coming to hang out with your favorite old guy on his birthday? Can I get you a drink?' I accepted, jumping on any opportunity to stall the conversation. Drew came back with a glass of soda that was still fizzing and reclaimed his spot.

"'So what are you going to do for your birthday?' I asked, trying to sound casual.

"'Woke up, went for a run, had breakfast with the girls, went for a swim, called my mom. They went out shopping and I was napping...'

"'Oh, sorry! I can go!' I said, embarrassed for just popping in.

"'Stop it. It's fine, I'm glad you are here. You okay?" he asked, a little more serious this time.

I took a deep breath. *Facing the fear is faster,* I thought.

"'Drew. I love CiCi,' I started. As a dad, I know now that Drew knew at that moment exactly what I was there for. But as a dad, you gotta make the guy squirm a little, right? So he sat there, expressionless, and let me ramble through my speech.

"'I come from nothing. I come from a mess and bad decisions and pain and darkness. But darkness is overcome by light, and the moment I first saw CiCi, it felt like the first time I had ever seen light. It was like seeing her made me understand what hope was. From the moment I met her, I wanted to be a better person for her. To make her proud. To make her happy. I can't picture my life without her. The things you've taught me, about being a shark, I take them and apply them so that I can be a shark for her. I want to be the one who fights for her, who supports her, who takes her where she is supposed to go. I want to be the one who protects her, who encourages her, who adds value to her life. I'm here today because I'd like your permission to ask CiCi if she would give me the honor of being her husband,' I said, finally breathing.

"Drew was silent—again, another classic dad move that you earn the right to after raising a daughter. When I had played out this scenario in my head, he had jumped up and hugged me and and said yes and we shared a toast and went out to play some golf. That is not what happened. He sat there, ran his fingers through his beard. He smiled at me, but looked away, lost in thought. I can't even imagine what that moment was like for him. I know one day it'll be me and it is something I won't be prepared for. Finally, he said something.

"'What do you notice?' he asked, 'About CiCi—what do you notice when you really *see* her? Not when you look at her, but when you *see* her?' he asked, seriously.

I wasn't ready for questions. I thought for a second and then responded, "'I see a giver. A selfless, patient, honest, independent, giving person who thinks about others before she thinks of herself. Someone who encourages other people; she makes people feel valued and heard and important. She loves fiercely,' I said, wondering if I should keep going.

"'As a father,' he said, looking deep into my eyes, 'it is my job to protect my daughter at all costs. When it comes to her, I would move mountains. I would give her my last breath. I would kill anyone who hurt her and do the time with a smile on my face. I know her. Like, know her, know her. And boy do I love her,' he said, glancing up at the framed pictures of younger CiCi on the wall.

"'The second the doctor puts your daughter in your arms, you understand your purpose. You understand your sole responsibility is to create a world where she feels safe, valued, loved, powerful, and capable. As a father, you know there will be a day when a boy realizes what you've known about your daughter for her entire life: that she is remarkable, irreplaceable, and a true gift. And you wonder what you'll do and say when that boy comes knocking, promising the world to the one person you would die for.' His voice cracked, and he looked back at me. I was so nervous. It was quiet for a while, but he continued. I didn't quite grasp what he was saying then, but when I became a dad to a daughter myself, I got it," Scotty said, choking up. Brittany got up and rubbed his back.

"Drew went on. 'As I held that seven-pound baby in the hospital, as I twirled her around on my feet in her princess dress the night before her first day of kindergarten, as I watched her turn into the incredible woman that she is today, there is no way I could have expected, hoped, that she would find a man like you. I knew she loved you a long time ago, and the only thing a man wants is for his daughter to find someone who sees who she truly is. And I know you do. I would be honored to have you as my son-in-law. Yes, yes, one hundred times yes, you have my permission to marry CiCi!' he said, wiping the tears from his eyes and jumping to his feet. I stood, and the tears came, and I fell into him like a little boy falls into his father. Drew put his hand on the back of my head and I wept into his shoulder. I wept for the dad who wasn't healthy enough to be there for me, for the woman I loved more than my own life, for this new father who saved me from who I might have become," Scotty said, looking over at Brittany, who was laughing and bawling at the same time, the way she always did when Scotty told this story. It still got her every single time.

> "You are the son I lost. God eased the pain and filled the void in my heart. You will not be my son-in-law, you will be my son-in-love."

"He told me, 'Scotty, God is good.

You are the son I lost. God eased the pain and filled the void in my heart. You will not be my son-in-law, you will be my son-in-love.'

"So we got it together: We did actually have a toast, and then I left because I knew the girls would be home soon from shopping. I shook Drew's hand as he walked me out and then I drove straight to my dad's house. My dad's truck wasn't in the driveway, and I was relieved. I walked straight in, gagged at the sight of old food in the sink, and went right back to my dad's bedroom. Beer bottles littered the floor, the room smelled like a mixture of marijuana and urine, and I was careful not to touch anything. I threw the laundry off the dresser and onto the floor to uncover a small wooden jewelry box. Years of dust and dirt made it a little hard to open, but when I got it open, it took my breath away. It still smelled like mom's old perfume, and her favorite little ladybug earrings were lying front and center. There were necklaces tangled together and a few dangly bracelets that I moved aside. I lifted the entire middle section to expose a hidden storage area underneath, and saw the ring right away. The simple silver band was shinier then I remembered, and the diamond on top seemed too flashy for Mom's style. But there was no doubt—this was it. I remembered watching my dad slide it off her finger at the funeral. I put the ring in my pocket, closed the jewelry box, and ran out of the house."

Paul thought about what Drew had said about how becoming a father helps you redefine your purpose. He had never thought of it that way before; he had always thought that being a dad was something that happened *to* him, a milestone that happened as a result of too much alcohol, a swanky hotel room, and a lot of lust. He became a dad because that is what you become when your wife got pregnant. But he realized now that being a dad isn't something that happens to you, it is something that you choose to become. *You may not get to choose to be a father, but you one hundred percent choose to be a dad. And for the past twenty odd years of Zach's life, I didn't choose to be a dad. I never felt that pull to protect someone, to look out for the best interest of someone regardless of the cost. I never had someone who I would move mountains for, who I truly cared for above myself. . .* Paul's mind was spinning.

"But he realized now that being a dad isn't something that happens to you, it is something that you choose to become."

The way Drew talked about CiCi, the way Scotty feels about Brittany, I've only felt those things about myself, Paul thought, sinking back into guilt and shame. Paul looked over at Scotty and tried to understand what Drew meant by not just *looking* at someone, but truly *seeing* them. He stared at Scotty and felt a tinge of jealousy. Scotty was eloquent, intelligent, funny, a good listener, a great storyteller. He was humble, a doting father, a loving husband, a hard worker, a successful business guy. *Everything that I pretend to be,* Paul thought, and for the first time acknowledged that his way of doing business, and relationships, and life, might not be the best way. The phrase Brittany said in the beginning of the day rang in his head: "You are who you hang out with." But if he wanted to be like Scotty, he'd have to do two things. Number one, he'd have to admit that Scotty had strengths that he didn't. The thought made his stomach hurt. Number two, he would have to put himself in a position to learn from Scotty, to surround himself with people like Scotty, who could identify his weaknesses and turn them into strengths. He felt like he would be sick again. *This is not going to be easy, get yourself together,* Paul thought. He was in a mental tug of war. *Can you teach an old dog new tricks?*

"I knew exactly where and how I wanted to propose, so a few weekends after the talk with Drew I asked for a Friday off and picked CiCi up for a surprise road trip. I took a picture of her as we were driving, her feet up on the dashboard, her hair falling on her shoulders. Those freckles, the sun setting behind her. I still have the picture. We arrived at Nags Head after dark and checked into our budget hotel. I waited for her to fall asleep before I got to work on my plan. I worked through the night, terrified she'd wake up and realize I was missing. I had been asleep for about two hours when my alarm went off at 3:30 a.m. It took some convincing, but she eventually got out of bed and followed me downstairs, through the parking lot and toward the water. She kept asking where we were going and commenting on how dark it was, but I just held her hand and told her to wait. I kept the lighthouse in sight, and moved quickly through the darkness toward it. As the sound of the ocean got louder, she noticed the tealight candles lining our path. She stopped in her tracks, but I pulled her along. We followed the trail of candles to the base of the lighthouse, where I had arranged dozens of tiny white candles in a circle. I leaned over and pressed play on my boombox; "Endless Love" by Lionel Richie began to play and we stepped into the circle of light.

"'CiCi, before you, my world was darkness. Utter darkness. Like this, all around us,' I began, my hands shaking. I took her hands in mine.

"'I picked 3:30 in the morning because they say it's always the darkest before dawn. This is the darkest part of the day, and every day before I met you was like this. I was consumed in the darkness, lost in it. But the first day I saw you, it was like that first candle back there—a tiny glimmer of light in my darkness. But each day we spent together, I felt like we were conquering the darkness. Each moment with you gave me the ability to see my next step. We've been together for 1,241 days,' I said, motioning to the candles. It took her a second to grasp what I was saying.

"'Did you line up 1,241 candles?' she shrieked, covering her mouth. I smiled. My back was sore from placing the candles, but I was grateful for the help of a few nightshift workers in getting it done.

"'You've been my light since day one. And this, this lighthouse, is what I want to be for you. A beacon of hope. A light when you're lost. A fortress, a place of protection and stability. I love you. CiCi May Peters, will you do me the honor of being my wife?' I asked, getting down on one knee and presenting my mom's engagement ring. She jumped up and down, cried, put her hands on my face, and kissed me. I slid the ring on her finger and held her. We danced to the music, swaying back and forth, kissing, laughing, talking. When we finally pulled apart, the sun was peeking up over the water. *Perfect timing.*

"CiCi has always been my light, and I strive every day to be the light for others," Scotty said, smiling. "But marriage is not easy. It's a commitment and a choice to get through the hard stuff together, just like you enjoy the good stuff together. We've faced plenty of hardships, but I keep thinking about what Coach used to say.

If it doesn't challenge you, it won't change you. Swim harder.

"Being the best husband I can be is a challenge. Finding ways to communicate better, to swallow my pride, to have the hard conversations without running off, to compromise even when I know I'm right—they're all challenging. But they change who I am as a person and as a husband. So I swim harder. I love harder, try harder, listen harder. I do the hard things because I know the result is worth it.

"If it doesn't challenge you, it won't change you. Swim harder."

"I used to swim harder until my lungs felt like they were going to burst. I'd swim harder until it felt like I tore a muscle. I'd swim harder because I knew it would make me a better swimmer. Same goes with every relationship we have, both personal and professional. We have to do the challenging things in order to change. We have to swim harder," Scotty said enthusiastically.

"The Sacred Six is how we all should SWIM. It's a blueprint of how to operate as a person of integrity and success. It's a code of honor to live up to; we will all come short, but the

Sacred Six is how we tell a real shark from everything else in the ocean. We all need to become sharks."

"The Sacred Six is how we tell a real shark from everything else in the ocean. We all need to become sharks."

Paul felt like Scotty had read his mind; that somehow Scotty could sense the internal struggle he was having with wanting to change but being reluctant to do what was challenging, simply because the work was hard. Paul was no stranger to hard work; he worked hard at everything he did. *But you do it for the wrong reasons,* Paul thought. *You work hard if it means recognition from someone else, if it is something you know you can excel in. But when it comes to addressing your own issues, or doing something that you'll never get external praise for, you hide. Like being a good dad. Like being a good, faithful husband.* Paul's mind raced. He started to realize that his hesitation in doing the hard work on himself stemmed from a deep-rooted place of insecurity and the belief that he wasn't worth the effort. He could point out the weaknesses in others all day long, but when it came to acknowledging his own in order to improve upon them, he froze. *This is why the thought of admitting to Scotty that you could learn a thing or two from him makes you want to vomit. Because it would mean admitting weakness, admitting doubt and failure. And then doing something about it. And if you try to do something about it and fail...* Paul thought, but shook away the thought. He struggled to put himself in a place of such vulnerability.

He could point out the weaknesses in others all day long, but when it came to acknowledging his own in order to improve upon them, he froze.

"One of the main things I took away from Drew's lessons about the shark, the suckerfish, and the parasite was that the relationship is pretty fluid between the three," Scotty said, pulling Paul out of his black hole of self-reflection.

"I was acting like a parasite when I punched that guy who was talking to CiCi. I was acting like a parasite when I was stealing from people to get money for drugs. I was a suckerfish when I finally let go of my pride and accepted the fact that admitting my weaknesses and striving to be like someone who clearly had it more together than I did was only going to benefit me," Scotty said, and Paul was certain Scotty could read his mind.

"I was a shark when I used my experiences to help others, when I put my wife's and daughter's needs above my own, when I ran my business with integrity and expected nothing less from my team. But it all starts with the willingness to see where you fall in this trifecta and taking the first step toward change. Sharks are flexible," Scotty said, glancing at everyone on the boat.

Paul could almost see the tiny angel sitting on his right shoulder and the mischievous devil standing on his left.

Just tell him you admire his strength, that you could learn a thing or two from someone like him, the angel whispered.

Abort! Abort! That's humiliating. Don't do that. Go read a self-help book if you need it. You can figure it out without with Mr. AC Tech making you feel like an idiot! the devil shouted.

It's not weakness. It's strength. Like Scotty said, just because you've been acting like a parasite doesn't mean that you are one forever. You can be a shark, the angel pleaded. Paul felt like he was going crazy.

You're a shark. You were one before you got on this boat and you'll be one after. Maybe not the same kind of shark, but a shark all the same. You get stuff done. It's fine. You've made it this far on your own, the red devil scolded.

"In life," Scotty continued, "we all must effectively manage the three types of people in order to be successful. Sharks, suckerfish, and parasites are the only three types of people in this world. Once we can manage them effectively, we can go far in life. We first must understand that we can be all of these people throughout the day, so we need to be humble as we engage others. We manage sharks differently than we manage suckerfish, and we manage parasites way differently than we manage suckerfish.

"We all must effectively manage the three types of people in order to be successful. Sharks, suckerfish, and parasites are the only three types of people in this world.… We first must understand that we can be all of these people throughout the day, so we need to be humble as we engage others."

"Sharks identify and respect other sharks, right? So this means you are aware of the people in your life who are your peers and are getting it done as well as or maybe even better than you. We all have good qualities, so we should always show respect to our peers. By giving sharks freedom to move throughout your life or business, you add strength to your team. Remember how the sharks in the tank at the aquarium just swam around together without killing each other? This is how you know you're surrounded by sharks. Everyone knows their role and their value and does not feel threatened or intimidated by greatness," Scotty said matter-of-factly.

"And then how do you manage the leeches?" Zach asked.

"The suckerfish. Not leeches, Zach, suckerfish. The suckerfish are managed in a separate way. They often crave direction and guidance, but once they find their spot, they're a vital part of the team and become sharks too, with the right support. They are eager to learn and need to be put in situations where they can connect with a shark and be mentored. They want to go places but are aware that they need someone else to help them get there. These people work best when they are challenged. They need their questions met with patience, and they work best when their loyalty and work ethic are acknowledged.

"These suckerfish aren't about getting a free ride. They're valuable members of the team who understand the power of mentorship and take in and are hungry to learn and grow. Imagine that a great company or organization should be a building full of sharks and suckerfish but not flunkies, 'yes men' or dead weight either. A suckerfish is nobody's flunky.

"Here is the truth: Great leaders influence; bad leaders rule. A shark should recognize a suckerfish's weaknesses or shortcomings and have a heart to help them grow and improve, knowing they are valuable. You should know this: Some sharks eat suckerfish. Sad but true, they see the suckerfish's weakness or shortcomings and feast on it, take advantage of it. Make sense? There is not much difference between a small shark and a giant parasite. Not much difference at all!

> "Here is the truth: Great leaders influence; bad leaders rule. A shark should recognize a suckerfish's weaknesses or shortcomings and have a heart to help them grow and improve, knowing they are valuable."

"That is the gap I see in this world that the Sacred Six can fix. We need more leaders who want to take suckerfish with them; you aren't successful unless you take others with you and allow them to feast, too."

> "You aren't successful unless you take others with you."

"And the parasites?" Zach shuddered. "How should we manage them?"

"Parasites are managed in a completely different way. Like we said before, in the ocean, the parasite is a parasite. They don't change and the goal of the suckerfish is to destroy them. In our case—"

"There's hope for the parasite," Paul chimed in, realizing it was his favorite phrase of the day.

"Right. Hope for the parasite. Our mission in managing them is not to destroy them; instead, managing parasites means being honest in your assessment, clear about your boundaries and expectations, and open-minded enough to offer a second chance. Parasites often aren't aware of how their behavior impacts others or the team and simply need to be called out in love about what they have to do to change. As we know, parasites are often a result of broken or a messy past that has robbed them of their ability to integrate successfully into a social or professional setting. Taking the time to get to know why parasites act the way they do is a first step in helping them change their ways. Parasitic people don't trust others, and there could be a good reason for that. That's why there is hope for a parasite—most people who act that way do it out of pain. Remember, hurt people hurt people.

"Parasites often aren't aware of how their behavior impacts others or the team, and simply need to be called out in love about what they have to do to change.... Taking the time to get to know why parasites act the way they do is a first step in helping them change their ways."

"But we know that parasites can quickly take down their host and that they are known for spreading death and disease everywhere they go, so they can't be left on their own. They can't be shoved in a back office or ignored in order to keep the peace. Parasitic-type people must be handled swiftly in order to maintain the health and balance of the team. They're hard to get rid of though, right? So they won't go without a fight. Your goal is not to fire every parasite and send them to suck the time, energy, and resources from another host; it is to help them evolve into a species that not only gives them a better chance to thrive but gives the company a better chance to thrive as well. However, it is important to know when enough is enough and to be proactive in removing a parasite that has no intention of changing," Scotty explained.

> "Parasitic people don't trust others, and there could be a good reason for that."

Brittany chimed in. "We are kind of covering this in one of my HR classes." She added, "HR departments deal with parasites all day. Sometimes you don't have to get rid of the person, but you must get rid of the attitude." Scotty winked at her, and his heart grew a little with pride.

I can't just say out loud, "Hey Scotty, can I be your suckerfish?" Paul thought to himself. *It sounds corny and would make me feel weak. But that is what needs to happen. If I'm going to redefine what it means to be a shark, I need to show some humility for once and latch on to…* Paul stopped. It all sounded too weird and creepy. It made him feel needy and submissive. He didn't like the feeling, so he tried to change his train of thought. But his mind kept coming back to the battle between what he needed to do and what he was comfortable doing. Admitting weakness and asking for help was so foreign to him, and the idea of doing it in front of his son was tough, even though it was the right thing to do. What if his son laughed at him? Or was embarrassed and thought that his dad was acting like a wimp for reaching out for help?

"So what happened to Drew?" Paul asked, desperate to switch the conversation and focus on something other than his own self-analysis.

"Ah. So sad. He got eaten by a shark," Scotty said in a somber voice.

"No way!" Paul said, whipping his head around to look at Scotty. Scotty couldn't help but smile. Everyone seemed to appreciate a little light-hearted humor after a long and very emotional day.

"Just kidding. He told me to tell people he got eaten by a shark, but I still can't do it with a straight face." Scotty smiled, playfully nudging Paul. Paul laughed.

"Something far less exciting. Cancer. He was diagnosed and died in the same year; it was quick. He was mad that it was cancer, because sharks are known for their impressive immune systems and their incredible ability to fight diseases. He said he wished it would be something more exciting like a shark attack or running into a burning building to save a cat. But apparently, cancer didn't know Drew was a shark. Pancreatic. Thankfully he didn't suffer very long, and we were all there. It was peaceful," Scotty said, still finding it hard to talk about. He continued, remembering that Drew made each of them promise to keep the movement going and not focus on the pain. "Drew just wanted each of us to keep his spirit alive in the way we lived our lives, and remember him for the good times, his corny humor, and, of course, the Sacred Six.

"I remember exactly where I was when CiCi called me and told me to drop everything. 'It's time,' she said, her voice shaking. I picked Brittany up from school and headed straight to Drew's; the hospital had released him to hospice, but Drew wanted to be home. He was awake but fading: his breathing was shallow and he was a skeleton, every bone in his body poking through his transparent skin. I just stood at the doorway. Frozen. With a shaky, thin finger, Drew pointed to the chair beside the bed. I sat.

"'Drew, I . . . ,' I started, choking up.

"'No, no. You don't. My turn,' he said, squeezing my hand. "'You're a shark. Everything you need is in the top drawer of the filing cabinet,' he said, taking a deep breath. 'Password to the lock is SWIM. It is yours. All of it. Take it and keep it going. Matter of fact, grow this company, Scotty. You can do it. Remember that we are a training and development company masquerading as an AC company. Raise that one to be a shark,' he whispered, nodding toward Brittany. 'I'm proud of you. I love you. I leave knowing the most precious thing in the world to me is safe and loved,' he said, smiling over at CiCi.

"'I'm tired. I've done a lot of swimming. I'm ready to stop swimming,' Drew said, and coughed. I knew what it meant, his reference to sharks and what happened when they stopped moving. CiCi began to sob and laid her head on her dad's chest. Brittany climbed into my lap. I looked at Drew at the end of his life and Brittany just starting hers, and realized how cyclical life really is.

"'You don't get to stop swimming," Drew said slowly. 'You have to keep moving. For me. For them. When you are a shark, you don't just swim, you SWIM. Tell 'em. Tell 'em I got eaten by a shark,' Drew said, taking breaths in between words. 'I'm tired,' he said softly, and shut his eyes. The hospice nurse came over and gently placed her two fingers on his wrist. She gave a sad smile, and I knew. He was gone. His motionless body just lay there, and we all stared. The biggest impact player I'd ever known, gone. He was not only a shark, Drew was a great white. I wrapped Drew in my arms and sobbed. My dad hadn't done his job, but God had sent me an angel to teach me how to be a man. A real man! I stood up and walked over to CiCi and held her. After that, it was all a blur. We took his ashes out on our boat and spread them in the ocean. It felt like the only appropriate place," Scotty said.

Tears streamed down Brittany's face, and she wiped them with her sleeve.

"To know and experience true love and leadership is priceless and life-changing. I know my life wasn't perfect and was hell early on, but I wouldn't change a thing. Because when I met Drew and became his suckerfish, it was like the pain of my childhood faded away and I was able to begin a new life, in the right way," Scotty said with confidence.

"To know and experience true love and leadership is priceless and life-changing."

Paul took a deep breath, clearly moved by the story.

Scotty cracked his knuckles and continued. "We had talked a few weeks after his diagnosis about me taking over the business, which is what he was referring to when he told me about the filing cabinet. He was so prepared—had everything already changed over to my name, notebooks full of client names and history, tips and tricks for AC repair, his business plan, his bank information, his computer we bought him, too. All of it. I saw right there on the line, gross revenue of $5,000,000. I had had no idea, because the company's success wasn't about the money. We were a business that operated like a family. When we were finally able to focus again, and I began to get the affairs in order, I was shocked at what Drew had left me with. He was very good with his money, brilliant, and left me to manage it all. I felt unfit for the job. But CiCi helped out a lot, and with plenty of trial and error, Sharks was running better than before. Every decision we make is run through the 'What would Drew do?' filter, and it helps us make smart decisions with integrity," Scotty said, smiling. "Now we are not only a $25,000,000 company, but we also have a great culture built on great core values that have been passed down. We don't focus on money, we focus on people. Like Drew always said, we are in the people business."

When Scotty stopped talking, the silence sent Paul's mind right back to his internal struggle. He still could not get past the fact that Scotty was the CEO of a $25,000,000 company. *Damn! I thought he was just a dumb AC tech*, Paul thought, running his fingers through his hair. Paul knew they were quickly getting close to shore, and if he wasn't intentional now about asking for help and learning from Scotty, he knew he never would. Scotty was the shark Paul had always thought he was, and he regretted thinking anything less of him. *How wrong I was about Scotty and what life is really about*, he groaned inside. *There's hope for the parasite, but it's not going to happen on its own. I have to do the challenging work to make a change. Scotty represents everything I want to be, everything I need to be. What a day! Maybe the best day of my life. It hurts, but this pain feels good. I know I'm a better man and I'm more excited than ever about my future,* Paul thought, and felt a smile creeping to his face. He could do this. No, he *had* to do this.

> *Scotty represents everything I want to be, everything I need to be. . . . I know I'm a better man and I'm more excited than ever about my future.*

"Hey, Scotty?" Paul said, breaking the silence. Scotty looked over at him. Paul's stomach flipped, his heart raced.

"I was doing some thinking, and I wanted to uh … It's just that … Well, ya see, I was thinking I could be your …," Paul stumbled, already regretting his questions. "I could be your fishing buddy, ya know, next time we do this," he said with a forced smile. The confusion on Scotty's face was obvious, and Paul felt foolish.

"Yeah man, that'd be cool. Maybe we can take my boat out next time," Scotty suggested.

Paul nodded and kicked himself for chickening out. Out in the distance, the marina came into view, a tiny speck on the horizon. Paul knew his time to finally step up and be intentional about doing something good was coming to a close. If he didn't do it now, not only would his future suffer, but so would his son's. If there was ever a time to step up and put someone else before himself, now was it. The fact that it was close to physically impossible for Paul to admit his weaknesses made him realize how much work he needed to do. One day of fishing had turned his world upside down, but in a good way.

Brittany and Zach started to clean up, putting things away to prepare to dock. It felt like everything was happening in slow motion; he could almost hear the seconds ticking down. The boat sped toward the shore, each building getting bigger as they got closer. Paul gripped the steering wheel and tapped his foot. Then, as if in slow motion, Scotty walked from the front of the boat straight to him. Scotty stood next to him and put his hand on his shoulder.

"Good day, eh?" Scotty asked, patting Paul's shoulder.

"Yeah, yeah. Didn't catch much, but still, it was a great day, Scotty. Learned a lot," Paul said, feeling nervous. It was silent for a little while. Paul counted down from 5.

5 … 4 … 3 … 2 …

"Plans for the rest of the weekend?" Scotty asked, interrupting Paul's countdown.

"Don't think so. Working, probably," he said, without even thinking. It was his go-to answer whenever anyone asked him what he was doing. Because it was all he did. Scotty nodded and stood silent. Paul felt like Scotty was just waiting for him to speak up, giving him the opportunity to take the step that everyone knew he needed to take.

"Scotty, man, I uhhh . . ." Paul took a deep breath. "I wanted to say sorry. Sorry for not being a good friend back then. Sorry for the way I thought about you. Treated you. I underestimated you. I really did. I learned that today," he said quickly. "You're not the guy I thought you were," Paul continued. "You deserve a lot more credit. You're a bigger man than I am," he said, surprised at how easy it felt to say. Scotty's eyes widened.

"You got it together. Great business, great family. You help people. You're happy. You are successful. You're a real shark, dude," Paul said, patting Scotty on the shoulder. It was getting easier.

"I could learn a thing or two from you. You know, about all this leadership stuff," Paul said, gesturing between them. "I thought I was a shark. Turns out I may have had it all wrong. Would love to . . . uhh . . ." Paul hesitated as he realized Zach was listening. Zach's stare made Paul lose his train of thought.

"Would love to hear more about what Drew taught you. Maybe learn to swim. Not swim like"—he motioned toward the water—"but, you know, swim swim. Swim," he said, confidently. Scotty smiled, and Paul wanted him to say something. Anything.

"Paul, man. Yes, of course. I see a shark in you. You've always had shark tendencies. We can learn a lot from each other. Yes." Scotty smiled, shaking Paul's hand, careful not to make it a huge deal or sound condescending. Scotty knew how much courage it must have taken for Paul to say those things, and he didn't want to ruin the moment.

Zach watched from afar, observing how his dad slowly opened up to Scotty and stopped dead in his tracks when the words *you're a bigger man than I am* escaped his mouth. Zach stood frozen, listening to his dad speak in a way he had never heard before. For a second it made Zach feel uncomfortable, but then it made him feel proud. He wondered if this was a sign that something Scotty had said stuck with him. It made him feel hopeful that there was change on the horizon for a real relationship with his dad. He was no longer confused, but hopeful that this was could be the first of many really great days with his dad.

"So let's just say someone was a parasite. Or maybe not a parasite but maybe they could work on being a better shark. What would their first step be?" Zach asked, trying to sound casual and general.

"Great question, Zach. I would say, hypothetically, that if you were a parasite, if you were acknowledging that you had these tendencies, it would be a good sign that your level of self-awareness is enough to help you transform into what you're totally capable of being. One of the first things I would suggest to a hypothetical parasite, or someone with these tendencies, would be to find a shark in your life. Find someone who has the qualities you admire. And when you find them, you have to tell them. That's the hard part. It can be weird and awkward and make you feel vulnerable, but you have to do it. The shark in your life needs to know that you are watching and willing to learn in order to most effectively teach you. That would be the first step," Scotty explained.

Paul felt a sense of relief. He had just taken the first step by finding the courage to tell Scotty he wanted to learn from him. He felt slightly more empowered.

"And then what would the hypothetical parasite do?" Paul asked eagerly.

"Well, the next part is not something you just do and check off a box. It's a shifting of the mindset. It is learning to put others before yourself, and this is only done through practice. It takes time. A lot of time. It happens slowly, and it can seem unnatural and uncomfortable at first, especially for a hypothetical parasite that has spent so much of his life … or her life, whatever, in a me-focused mindset. This happens when you reach out and apologize for wrongdoings, when you own up to mistakes, when you right wrongs. It can take years, your whole life even, to truly master this step. But you do other things simultaneously to become a shark. It all kind of happens at the same time. It's a change in your mindset and your lifestyle. It's like you've always known how to swim, but this is being taught to SWIM," Scotty explained.

> "It's a shifting of the mindset. It is learning to put others before yourself, and this is only done through practice."

The boat was quickly approaching the shore, and Scotty could begin to make out the buildings and the yachts bobbing in the water. All of a sudden, a loud dinging sound startled all of them, and the engines started to sputter.

"No, no, no, no, no!" Paul yelled, banging his fists on the steering wheel. Scotty followed Paul's gaze to the flashing gas light indicator. The boat slowly came to a stop as the engines halted.

"We're out of gas?" Brittany asked, peering over her dad's shoulder to check the gas indicator.

"Sure are. Damnit," Paul said, embarrassed and unsure of what to do. He knew he didn't have any backup gas tanks because he had yet to add them to his new boat. The four of them glanced out at the marina, so close yet so far away. Scotty pulled his phone out of his pocket and texted CiCi to let her know about the situation. Scotty's phone beeped, indicating that his battery was low.

"I don't have service," Brittany said, holding up her phone.

"Me either," said Zach, tossing his phone onto the padded captain's chair.

The boat bobbed in the water, and the sudden chill made Scotty realize that the sun was quickly setting. He weighed his options, checked his phone, which mocked him with more beeps, and looked around for help.

"Mayday, mayday," Paul barked into the boat's radio. "We ran out of gas. We're stranded!" he said urgently. Scotty chuckled at Paul's lack of radio etiquette, as this hardly qualified as a mayday situation. They could see the shore; they were not in any imminent danger. The only sound on the radio was static, and Paul called out again. Finally, a grainy voice came out over the speaker.

"Is that you, Paul?" laughed the voice on the other end. "You ran out of gas?" the voice asked. Paul rolled his eyes before responding.

"Hiya, Chris. Yes, we ran out. We're about four hundred yards from shore. Can someone help us out?"

"We had a small vessel capsize out in open water, so all our rescue boats are on that. May be a while before we can get out to you. Everyone okay?"

"A while? How long? Can't you just get someone? I just bought this boat this weekend. You don't have a system in place for this?" he barked, his voice escalating. "What kind of marina doesn't have the personnel to help someone who just bought a $400,000 bo—" Paul stopped. He looked sheepishly over at Scotty, who was watching him, arms crossed and eyebrows raised. Paul felt his face get red.

"You know what, Chris? It's actually just fine. We can wait. We've got sandwiches. Thanks. Keep us updated?" Paul said, softening his tone. Scotty smiled approvingly. Paul sat back in the captain's chair and put his feet up. He thought about what Scotty had said earlier that day about sharks never going backward. He realized how easy it was for him to fall back to his old ways, to revert to old strategies and habits, how easy it was to go back even after a whole day of forward movement. For a second he felt defeated, but the approving look on Scotty's face after Paul changed his tone let him know that it was okay.

He realized how easy it was for him to fall back to his old ways, to revert to old strategies and habits.

Scotty surveyed the situation. He was curious, so he calculated the distance from the boat to the shore, estimated the time it would take for the rescue boats to get back to them, and made a decision. He slipped his shoes off and put them under the seat. He took his car keys and now-dead phone out of his pockets and slipped them in the pocket of Brittany's bag. He lifted his shirt over his head and threw it down by his shoes. He was a little scared to do it, with the sun setting and the fact that he hadn't swum that far since high school—and always in lakes, never in the ocean.

"What in the world?" Brittany yelled, her eyes wide.

"Facing fear is faster. I'll just swim. I can make it. Then I can get help faster. It could be hours before they can help us. Maybe I can grab a gas can and borrow a wave runner and come back. I'll figure it out. It's better than sitting here and waiting. I have to do something," he said confidently. Thankfully the tide was pushing the boat closer to the dock.

Scotty climbed over the side of the boat and stood on the diving platform. To his surprise, he felt someone next to him. Paul, shirtless and in all of his muscled glory, was standing right next to him.

"Like old times?" he asked playfully. Scotty was speechless. He wasn't sure if he was touched by this sentimental gesture or annoyed that Paul had to make everything a competition.

"You don't have to. You can stay with the kids. I got it, you can just... Paul, this isn't the lake in Lake City, you know. There are real sharks here."

"When you are a shark, you don't just swim, you SWIM!" Paul said. He paused and then yelled, "I am a shark, too" and dove headfirst into the cold water. Scotty looked back at Brittany, who looked flabbergasted at how the situation had quickly developed. She threw her hands up in defeat and gave a reluctant smile. Scotty dove in and pushed with everything he had to catch up with Paul. Scotty hoped that although he didn't spend as much time in the weight room as Paul apparently did, his regular swimming routine would work to his advantage in this moment.

Scotty could see the details in the wood of the dock as he approached. Paul was an arm's length ahead of him, inching closer to the silver ladder that hung off over the side. *Swim harder,* Scotty thought and found a strength deep down inside of him to kick harder and push harder.

Paul could feel Scotty gaining on him. His arms didn't slice the water like they used to, and his breathing techniques were rusty. *This ain't high school anymore,* he thought. When Paul stepped onto the diving platform, he had envisioned diving gracefully into the water and gliding toward the dock with Scotty in his wake, like old times. Scotty felt himself start to panic. *This is not what I thought was going to happen,* Paul thought. *He's passing me. A cramp. I'll get a cramp and have to stop. I'll swim back to the boat,* he thought as he slowed down, trying to figure out an excuse to back out of the challenge. He knew he wasn't going to win. *Back,* Paul thought, *sharks don't swim backward. They don't go back to who they were once they know better,* he thought. He took a deep breath, found a focal point on the dock, and pushed each muscle in his body forward with purpose.

Slowly, with the dock approaching, Scotty passed Paul and threw his hands up on the dock. Paul grabbed on just 20 seconds after. The two pulled themselves up onto the dock, and Scotty put his hand up to give a high five. The two slapped hands and Paul waited for Scotty to boast and brag about winning, but he didn't. They both looked out into the water, and to their surprise, Paul's boat was cruising toward them with Brittany behind the wheel. Zach was waving something in his hands and laughing. As the boat slowed down to approach the dock, Paul and Scotty realized what it was. A gas can. Zach must have found a spare in a storage compartment on the boat.

"You son of a…" Paul laughed, quickly grabbing the lines and helping secure the boat to the dock. The sun disappeared below the horizon.

"What in the world?" CiCi exclaimed, running down the dock, approaching the four of them with a gas tank in hand, "You SWAM?" she asked, confused. She looked over at Brittany, who smiled and shrugged. Cici knew that if Brittany was smiling, everything was okay.

"How'd it go? Catch anything? Good day?" she asked, shifting her eyes from each person to get some sort of idea about how the day had gone.

"CiCi. Paul Gray. So nice to see you again after all these years!" Paul said, putting his hand out to shake hers. She ignored his hand and hugged him as she always did. "Great to see you again after all these years. Great guy you have here, this Scotty boy. Really enjoyed our day, he's really matured since high school," he said, patting Scotty on the back. "This day was unbelievable, Scotty!" He chuckled.

"Listen, I'm freezing, we're gonna head home," Paul said, shivering. "Scotty, thank you so much for today. I really look forward to hanging out more and learning a few things from you. Real shark, eh?" he said, looking over at CiCi. She smiled a confused smile because there is no way he could know about how much sharks meant to this family. Everyone said their goodbyes and Paul and Zach started walking down the boardwalk toward their car, until Paul stopped and turned around.

"CiCi! I'll be celebrating Drew's big day tomorrow! Happy birthday, Drew!" Paul shouted and turned the corner, out of sight. CiCi looked up at Scotty and raised her eyebrows in even more confusion, waiting for an explanation. "You better tell me everything," she said with a smile. Scotty locked her pinky with his and headed toward the parking lot.

He took a deep breath, thoughts of the events of the day swirling in his head. He leaned down to kiss the top of her head. "CiCi, I'm so glad that you are my shark and I am your suckerfish," Scotty said.

"Now, Scotty, how many times do I have to tell you that you are the shark and I am your suckerfish?" Cici sighed. They spoke in corny and obvious flirty voices.

"Caught a big one today, CiCi," Scotty began. "I battled Moby Dick all day, but we got 'em in the Sacred Six boat," Scotty said, putting an arm over Brittany's shoulder, thankful to be back on land with his two favorite girls.

"So today Paul learned to SWIM," Scotty began.

The Sacred Six

Sharks never stop moving forward.
Sharks never look down; they always look up.
Sharks are always curious and always learning.
Sharks always respect their environment and recognize other sharks.
Sharks are always flexible.
Sharks always elevate their suckerfish to new levels.

ACKNOWLEDGMENTS

I want to recognize and acknowledge a whale shark in my life that heard me talk about the Shark and the Suckerfish for the first time on stage: **Mark Victor Hansen**, one of the greatest authors ever. You told me that I was onto something. Coming from you, that means a lot of chicken soup to me. To hear an author of your caliber validate me was a life changer.

Brian Buffini, OMG! You told me you were going to help me, and you did. You not only told me to go for the book, you also helped me find Wiley. And it was on your stage where I talked about this book concept for the very first time. Without you or a Buffini event there would be no book. Thanks for letting me be your six-five, 300-pound suckerfish.

About the Author

Walter Bond made it to the NBA, but he didn't stop there. Where many would consider a career with the Utah Jazz, Detroit Pistons, and Dallas Mavericks one of life's greatest achievements, Walter saw it as a jumping-off point, a catalyst that launched him into what he was made to do. His experience on and off the court prepared him for a thriving career in business coaching, mentorship, and public speaking.

His journey to the NBA was not an easy one, but instead of seeing obstacles, Walter saw opportunity. While some may have complained about being on the bench as a college basketball player, Walter used it as an opportunity to hone in on the fundamentals every team needs to be successful. It was this mind shift, these simple yet powerful concepts, that has allowed Walter to reach massive audiences, long after his days on the court were over.

Walter weaves both inspirational anecdotes and action steps together in his engaging storytelling style and commands the audience with confidence. His relentless commitment to helping get entrepreneurs, business leaders, sales teams, and eager employees to the next level is what sets him apart from the rest.

Walter is far more than a former NBA player. He is a renowned business coach, an author, a high-profile speaker, a business owner, a father, a husband, and a friend. He is a breath of fresh air for businesses across the country that are eager to get to the next level.